at HBCUs

Cultivating Institutional
Relationships
to Positively Impact Alumni Giving

DEREK C. HENSON, PH.D.

Edited by SaFiya D. Hoskins, Ph.D.

Copyright © 2014 Derek C. Henson

Published by: Ubiquitous Press

All rights reserved.

ISBN-13: 978-0692275627
ISBN: 0692275622

DEDICATION

To the memory of my mother, Jnell Henson, who has always been my biggest fan, and closest friend.

In remembrance of my father, Charles Henson, who passed away the day I submitted my application for the doctoral program at JSU. I miss you.

Also, to my aunt, Maxine Johnson, for starting the family tradition of attending HBCUs.

Finally, to my siblings, Vickie, Shaun and Monica, each of whom attended an HBCU.

CONTENTS

	Acknowledgments	i
1	Alumni Giving: an Overview	1
2	Significance of Study	9
3	Methodology	15
4	Historical Context	18
5	Alumni Influences	27
6	Altruism	32
7	Management and Alumni Relations	37
8	Alumni Perceptions	42
9	Qualitative Analysis	48
10	Emergent Themes	58
11	Altruism in Effect	74
12	Relations and Socialization	84
13	Fundraising and Alumni Giving	100
14	Discussion and Conclusions	114
15	Implications for Policy and Practice	123
	References	131

ACKNOWLEDGMENTS

I would like to first thank God for giving me the strength
to complete this research and the Ph. D. degree.
For their respective contributions
I would like to acknowledge:
Dr. Walter L. Crockett, Dr. Neari F. Warner,
Dr. Walter A. Brown, Dr. Hilliard L. Lackey,
Dr. Jeton McClinton, Dr. Leonard Williams,
Dr. Andrea Mayfield, Dr. Bernard Turner,
Ms. Keisha Earnest, Mrs. Lora Thompson,
Ms. Vicky Lewis-Penn,
Pastor Whalum and the New Olivet Baptist Church.

Special thanks to Dr. SaFiya D. Hoskins.

1 ALUMNI GIVING: AN OVERVIEW

Although rich in history and legacies, many Historically Black Colleges and Universities (HBCUs) have struggled financially to maintain their existence (Boulard, 2001; Chronicle of Higher Education, 2003; Evan, Evans, Evans, 2002). A number of research studies on funding for HBCUs report that the primary funding sources are governmental entities, churches and philanthropists (Chronicle of Higher Education, 2003; Gasman, Baez, Drezner & Sedgwick, et. al, 2007; Strout, 2004). However, the Council for Aid to Education (2008) and Yates (2001) report that the leading source of revenue for most institutions of higher education is alumni. Hunter (1999) reports that the majority of HBCUs strive to develop strong financial development plans and support for fund-raising campaigns. However, <u>US News and World Reports</u> (2006, 2007, and 2008) reported that the average alumni giving rates at HBCUs is less than 12 %.

Many wealthy elite Predominately White Institutions (PWIs) have established family legacies of contributing to their alma maters, whereas HBCU alumni have not had that luxury (Ramsey, 1992). This is evident with the most recent declarations of colleges and universities endowment funds. The university endowment funds of Harvard, Yale, Princeton and Stanford have been leaders in reported annualized returns of 15.2% and 17.2 %, with staggering stockpiles of $34 billion, $18 billion, and $14 billion (CAE, 2008; Cech, 2008; Michael, 2007). Yet, these institutions are still ambitious in maintaining strong fund-raising strategies and campaign drives to sustain and increase new donors and strong fundraising results. Recently, Stanford began a $4.3 billion dollar campaign, which is reportedly the largest fund raising campaign in higher education history (CAE, 2008; Cech, 2008; Michael, 2007).

In February 2008, the Council for Aid to Education (CAE) released its yearly study on contributions to colleges and universities. It reported that charitable contributions to colleges and universities are up this past year from 6.3 %, an average of approximately $30 billion dollars. These results are based on the annual Voluntary Support of Education (VSE) survey. This report claims that this is the highest rate in recent years (CAE, 2008). The top twenty institutions have a combined total fundraising for donors of 7.66 billion dollars, which surmounts to 25.8 % of all donations made to colleges and universities. The Council for Aid to Education (2008) also claims that the wealthiest colleges and universities set the national alumni giving trends. Ironically, CAE (2008) also reports that alumni giving is down by 1.5 % in 2007, but alumni giving contributions remain consistent at 16.5 %, which is an increase from 2005. The study also reports that the top 20 institutions are responsible for 25% to 29 % of all alumni donations and that those alumni participation numbers are down mainly due to the number of alumni being produced which brings the national age average down (CAE, 2008).

According to the existing literature, financial instability is the most reported problem of many Historically Black Colleges and Universities. Several HBCUs have faced probation and the loss of accreditation because of their financial accounting practices and portfolio instability. Recent examples of these sanctions include the loss of accreditation at Morris Brown, Knox, and Barber Scotia Colleges (Southern Association of Colleges and Schools, 2008). More recently, the lens of scrutiny has come across Texas Southern University, Lemoyne Owen College, Fisk University and Grambling State University. All of the aforementioned schools faced some type of financial crisis or accountability of how funds had been allocated and used (Chronicle of Higher

Education, 2003; Gasman, Baez, Drezner & Sedgwick, et. al, 2007; Southern Association of Colleges and Schools, 2002). Under the leadership of its first female president, Dr. Neari F. Warner, Grambling State University successfully redeemed its academic status with SACS. LeMoyne Owen College recently bounced back from a probationary accreditation status after ultimately raising over $4 million dollars in pledges. It is not certain how much of this $4 million dollars was pledged by alumni (Journal of Blacks in Higher Education, 2007).

Dr. Hilliard Lackey (2008) stated recently in his article *All Supporters Are Not Members*,

The average Jackson State University graduate makes $39,000 annually which equates to $3,300 per month. The average household income for JSU grads tops $70,000. The average Jacksonian who donates, makes an annual gift of $250 to JSU but only 5% of alumni give. There are estimated 70,000 graduates and former students of Jackson State University scattered around the globe but only 3,000 pay alumni dues ($50) and only 3,500 make financial contributions to the University….. Still Jackson State University which ranks 1st, 2nd and in the top ten of most HBCU categories is off the bottom end of the charts when it comes to alumni giving (p. 10).

Cole (2008) reported that since the Civil Rights Movement, not only have HBCUs had to contend with Pre-dominantly White Institutions for students, but they have also had to struggle with continuous underfunding, which has led to some instances of accreditation issues. This lack of funding has also led to deteriorated campuses and infra-structures. The disparity of HBCUs alumni giving continues to erode and many media reports question the strength of HBCU alumni giving.

Although Predominately White Institutions enroll more African Americans numerically, Historically Black Colleges and Universities consistently grant more degrees to African-Americans than majority white institutions. Even with these graduation rates, there continues to be a disparity in increasing alumni giving results at HBCUs (CAE, 2008; Nealy, 2008, UNCF, 2008). The United Negro College Fund (UNCF) organization reports that of the 105 HBCUs listed in the United States, these organizations produce almost one quarter of African Americans with baccalaureate degrees (UNCF, 2008). The U.S. Department on Education (2008) reports that there are nearly 2.2 million African Americans enrolled in degree granting institutions.

According to a report released by CAE (2007), charitable contributions to colleges and universities increased in 2007, while alumni giving decreased, which reportedly includes a 6 % drop at Historically Black Colleges and Universities. While predominately white institutions (PWI) have enjoyed years of alumni giving, historically black colleges and universities have lagged behind in cultivating their alumni to give substantially and consistently (CAE, 2008; Cohen,

1998; Fields, 2001). Nealy (2008) and CAE (2008) reported that the average alumni donation from a PWI graduate is $1,195.00 as compared to a $475.00 donation for a HBCU graduate.

Ward (2004) and Scott (2001) posit that most studies on fundraising strategies are marketed for the majority white alumni audiences. Friedmann (2003) proposed that student alumni associations, pre-alumni groups, student foundations, and how student participation in these groups influenced and increased alumni donations and involvement. Friedmann's (2003) conceptual framework was based on social learning theories, particularly addressing building pro-social behavior through group participation. However, the study does not reveal whether or not data were collected and analyzed on historically black colleges and universities.

Most studies on alumni giving are monolithic and one-sided with the emphasis placed on donors. There are few theoretical studies addressing the dichotomous relationship building between development officials and alumni donors (Friedmann, 2003; Ward, 2004). Therefore, the primary problem that was addressed in the study was to what extent are institutions cultivating relationships that will produce financially active alumni at HBCUs. Since Historically Black institutions award the majority of degrees to Black students, it is imperative that the doors of these institutions remain open.

The purpose of this study was to determine if

HBCUs are cultivating potential relationships with future alumni by promoting altruistic, pro-social behavior through student or group involvement. Friedmann (2003) documented Schervish's (1993) communities of participation and how student participation in these groups may encourage pro-social behavior that could ultimately lead to increased alumni donor support and involvement. Communities of participation have been defined as the process of socialization and how individuals relate to their self- identified groups which in turn could possibly build pro-social behavior (altruism) (Schervish, 1993; Friedmann, 2003).

This study examined how HBCUs are cultivating alumni to become long term donors. Therefore, the purpose of this study is to contribute to the body of literature about perceived institutional relations and alumni giving, specifically pertaining to HBCU's or alumni.

The following research questions drive the study:

1. What are HBCUs doing to cultivate alumni relationships during the student's undergraduate years to create a feeling of involvement with the university and to become active alumni donors after graduation?
2. What are alumni affairs officers and other fund raising officers doing to encourage individuals or group participation that will

enhance alumni giving at HBCUs?
3. What fund raising strategies are HBCUs using to build successful alumni relationship and management systems?

2 SIGNIFICANCE OF STUDY

This study contributes to the body of literature on HBCUs institutional relations and alumni giving. Ayers & Associates (2002) reported that the largest group of donors to higher education is alumni and that from 2000 – 2001 that group produced $6.8 billion dollars in donations or about 28.2 % of total donations. This study also indicates that this group is perhaps the most under-tapped and under- developed group of donors. Their study also suggests that most institutions too often ask for donations before even developing any form of relationship with the alumni donor and neither was cultivation in preparation for future donations done before the alumnus graduated (Ayers & Associates, 2002). Baker (2004) and Reaves (2006) suggest presented research that there are numerous factors that influence African American alumni to give or not give back financially to their alma maters. This study also identified areas that need further research such as the way schools communicate with alumni. The Council for Aid to Education's Voluntary education support survey study presents compelling evidence that alumni donations are consistent, particularly at elite schools; yet, it does not give significant information on how the elite institutions have continued to raise funds that they may not necessarily need at the current time (CAE, 2008).

The Council for Aid to Education (2008) surmised that the top twenty institutions with billion and million dollar endowments set the trends and patterns for all higher education donors and alumni giving. However, according to previous studies findings on HBCUs fund raising, this is not the case as it pertains to HBCUs. As mentioned earlier, the average alumni giving rate is less than 12 % for all HBCUs with some institutions having as little as two percent of alumni giving (CAE, 2008; Powell, 2008; US News and World Report, 2008). The recent decline in the economy and federal, state funding has increased the search for funding from alumni, corporations and foundations, which have also faced financial losses (Allen & Jewel, 2002; Boulard, 2001; Strout, 2004; Turner, 2001; Rowland, 1997). However, CAE, (2006; 2007) reports that the top three sources of voluntary support comes from alumni (27.8%), corporations (16.1 %) and foundations (28.6%).

According to a study released by the *Journal of*

Blacks in Higher Education (2000), many African – American alumni do not give back for a variety of reasons such as, a lack of tradition of higher education philanthropy among black families as compared to white counterparts, which have sent generations off to college. There have been numerous studies on alumni and their giving patterns as well as several books on marketing to alumni and studies completed on factors that influence alumni giving rates; yet, there is a lack of research on methods to increase alumni giving at Historically Black Colleges and Universities (Ward, 2004).

Previous studies have focused on factors that encourage or deter alumni giving among various groups. These studies have divulged information on gender, racial, socio- economic status and group participation (Baker, 2004; Reaves, 2004; Ward, 2004). These particular demographics have reported various intrinsic and extrinsic motivators for alumni giving or not giving financially. Consequently, most of the studies do not identify significant factors that have consistently been most beneficial to any particular institution or group (Baker, 2004; Reaves, 2004; Ward, 2004).

Other studies have also conducted comparison analysis on black and white alumni giving rates, factors of influence, and various motivators for these two groups. These studies have also compared gender, socio economic status and time since graduation as indicators of giving rates between the two racial groups (Baker, 2004; Reaves, 2004; Scott, 2001; Ward, 2004).

There are some HBCUs that report higher alumni giving rates, such as Howard University, Spelman College and Morehouse College, but most public HBCUs do not compare or even reach these schools' rates. (CAE, 2008; Powell, 2008; US News and World Report, 2008; Nealy, 2008). Table 1 below was revised to reflect those institutions that have predominantly black enrollments as well as the HBCUs that meet the governmental mandate of HBCUs created or founded by1964.

Table 1 – HBCUs – Top Fundraising Institutions

Sorted List Based on Grand Total

Historically Black Colleges and Universities / Highest 1500 / FY2007

1	Morehouse College (Atlanta, GA)	$34.62 million
2	**Univ. of Texas at El Paso (El Paso, TX)	$16.73 million
3	**Cuyahoga Community College (Cleveland, OH)	$9.95 million
4	North Carolina A & T State University (Greensboro, NC)	$9.05 million
5	Morehouse School of Medicine (Atlanta, GA)	$6.52 million
6	Meharry Medical College (Nashville, TN)	$6.45 million
7	Winston-Salem State University (Winston-Salem, NC)	$3.86 million
8	Fisk University (Nashville, TN)	$3.10 million
9	North Carolina Central University (Durham, NC)	$1.88 million
10	Prairie View A&M University (Prairie View, TX)	$1.79 million

**Does not meet the HBCU mandate but have pre-dominantly Black enrollments.

According to Gasman et al., (2007) and Boulard (2001), research studies on recent trends at HBCUs reported that the recent problems with accreditation and financial instability at HBCUs are primary factors in the development of strong fundraising activities. However, not much information on new trends in helping HBCUs increase alumni giving rates was presented. Philanthropists and alumni see charitable giving as a capitol investment market. The first step in performance philanthropy is based on data gathering of results and not simply what an organization needs. Performance philanthropy gives organizations the opportunity to get additional benefits as well. It can maximize results that will encourage additional charitable investments (Thurman, 2006). Donors who understand and are able to track the use of their donations are more likely to become a more consistent donor and committed to the philanthropic efforts of the organization (Thurman, 2006).

This study is significant in that it will contribute to the body of knowledge relating to alumni donor relations. The information generated by this study should enable alumni affairs and development officers to better understand the relationship between alumni and their alma maters as it relates to donor relations and assist in the development of policies and procedures that can be used in daily management practices.

3 METHODOLOGY

The methodology utilized by this study was qualitative in nature. This approach was used due to the style of questions that were employed. The interviewer used open – ended questions to illicit detailed responses (Marshall & Rossman, 2006).The study consisted of alumni from two HBCUs. The study interviewed financially active alumni and non-active alumni, in order to have a better understanding of students becoming financially active alumni. The researcher also interviewed current development and alumni affairs officers to gather data on trends or practices. Participants in the study will be selected using the simple criterion selection process which will follow the tenets of random selection (Creswell, 2003).

The following terms are defined for the purpose of this study:

Active alumni donor: alumni members that have

contributed financially to their respective alma maters within the last five years.

Non Active Alumni donor: any alumni that have not contributed financially to respective alma mater within at least the last five years or longer.

Philanthropy is defined as any financial contribution or artifacts and property that have a significant value that can be converted to a monetary value.

Historically Black Colleges and Universities (HBCUs): according to the governmental distinction of historically black colleges and universities, these institutions must have been established before 1964.

Predominately White Institutions (PWIs): for the purpose of this study are institutions with majority white student enrollments.

Altruism: is defined as the act of voluntary contributions or services without the intentions of receiving anything in return.

Socialization: the inter-active relationships through personal or humanistic contact that conveys the roles and rules of each society (Weidman, 1989).

Cultivation: the development and relationship building techniques of alumni donors.

This study is delimited to alumni and alumni affairs / development officers from two historically black colleges and universities located in the southern region of the United States. The two institutions chosen are both four year institutions – one is a public institution and one is a private institution.

One of the limitations of the study is that the data

compiled was based on a very limited sample. The absence of generalizability from the particular environment of participating individuals was considered as another limitation of the study. The sample size is fairly small considering the size and population of the institutions being considered in the research. Another limitation of the study is that the researcher depended on the honesty and integrity of the respondents and their recollection of past events. The researcher had to make the assumption that the responses are fairly correct. Therefore the findings of this study may not be readily generalized to other institutions.

4 HISTORICAL CONTEXT

From the opening of the first Historically Black College of Cheyney State College in Cheyney, Pennsylvania in 1832, the issues of financial stability have often come into play (Brown, 2003, Allen & Jewel, 2001). After the Civil War, America saw a proliferation of Historically Black Colleges and Universities develop throughout the country; over 200 or so Historically Black Colleges and Universities opened their doors (Brown, 2003, Roebuck & Murty, 1989). These colleges were opened to educate the newly- freed slaves, considering there were well over four million freed slaves after the Emancipation Proclamation was signed into law (Allen & Jewel, 2001; Brown 2007; Rowland, 1997).

By the 1920s it was estimated that almost 10,000 African Americans held college degrees; today there are over 3.8 million African Americans with bachelor's degrees. In 2002, reportedly over 170,000 African Americans had enrolled in graduate schools across the United States. This is roughly estimated as 8.4% of the total number of students enrolled in graduate schools (Journal of Blacks in Higher Education, 2007). Nichols (2004) reported that Historically Black Colleges and Universities had produced 48% of all Black computer scientists, 43 % of all of physical scientists and 48% of all Black teachers. This surmounts to over 300,000 black college graduates every ten years.

The National Center for Education Statistics reported in 2007 that Historically Black Colleges and Universities accounted for only 3% of all of the United States' institutions of higher learning; however, they currently confer over 23.6% of all baccalaureate degrees. In the concentrated areas of mathematics, physical, biology and agriculture fields Historically Black Colleges and Universities account for more than 40% of bachelors' degrees earned by African Americans. HBCUs also confer 13.1% of master's degrees.

Reaves (2006) surmises that historically, HBCUs were forced to conform to the desires of white philanthropists, who funded their institutions and that several private, liberal arts HBCUs were forced to adopt the principles of a technical model of education in order to continue to receive donations and financial support. Today, the private (as well as public) HBCUs acquiesce to the government, corporations and foundations to which they are dependant for financial resources.

The Morrill Act of 1890 was the financial beginning for some of the first HBCUs. This Act of Congress mandated that the federal government would deny funds or land to states that would deny admissions of Black students or if they would not create separate but equal quality. In essence, this created what would become known as dual systems of higher education, one system for whites and one system for blacks. This law is still affecting Black colleges today considering the recent 2004 decision in the Jake Ayers' case in Mississippi (Cohen, 1998, Brown, 2003, Roach, 2007, Roebuck & Murty, 1989, Rudolph, 1998).

Evan, Evans & Evans (2002) argued, "The HBCU was not designed to succeed; rather, they were established to appease Black people or to serve as 'holding institutions' so that Black students would not matriculate in Historically White Colleges and universities." (p.3). Fortunately, most HBCUs have excelled and continued to prove this prediction wrong (Nichols, 2004).

The Church

The church was and continues today to be a consistent supporter of HBCUs, since the inception of Black colleges. Almost all of the 103 HBCUs have or had some affiliation with the church or religious sects. From donated land, use of facilities, and /or financial contributions, the church has had some influence, particularly in the Black Community (Cohen, 1998, Brown, 2003, Yates, 2001). From Jackson State University's beginnings as a Normal School founded by the American Baptist Home Mission Society to Dillard University's Methodist Episcopal influences or St. Augustine Colleges' in Raleigh, N. C. Episcopalian roots, religious influences continue to be a part of the financial threads of HBCUs (Cohen, 1998; Roach, 2007; Powell, 2004; Yates, 2001). The church at one time in our history was the only place where groups of Blacks could gather freely. This also set the tone for HBCUs to be the beacon of the Black social climate (Brown, 2003, William & Kritsonis, 2006).

Williams & Kritsonis (2006) posit that most African Americans are taught about giving back through their church affiliations. Black pastors and preachers have consistently encouraged their members to support the work of their churches; subsequently, this meant supporting black colleges with direct donations or by sending church members children to college. Many of these prominent pastors were educated in these same institutions (Williams and Kritsonis, 2006; UNCF, 2008).

Judicial Influences

Even before Brown v. Board of Education in

1954, there were other legal challenges concerning higher education. In 1950, Sweatt v. Painter dealt with Texas Law Schools being separate but equal, and McLaurin v. Oklahoma State Regents for Higher Education argued that a black doctoral student be given the same rights as other non- black students. The Brown case, however, began the tearing down of walls of separate but equal facilities (Cohen, 1998). The 1956 court case of Florida ex. vel Hawkins v. Board of Control extended the Brown ruling to colleges and universities. Yet, it would still be years before desegregation would begin in many southern states, since there was no specific time limit given to the states to comply with the ruling. A specific time would not be given until the 1969 case of *Alexander v. Holmes County Board of Education*, in which the U. S. Supreme Court imposed immediate desegregation of all schools (Roebuck & Murty, 1989).

The 1970 lawsuit brought by the NAACP on behalf of *Adams v. Richardson* took nearly seven years before a court in 1977 mandated that the Department of Health, Education and Welfare develop desegregation guidelines to tackle states that operated dual segregated, higher education systems. Many southern states still operate dual systems by default of the court order. One of the prevailing clauses of the court order was that states could not close predominately black schools to satisfy desegregation mandates (Roebuck & Murty, 1989). Another prime example of long court battles is the 1975 lawsuit filed by Jake Ayers, Sr., against the State of Mississippi on behalf of his son, Jake Ayers, Jr., a student at Jackson State University. The Ayers case was still debated as recently as May 2004. In essence, the Ayers case sought to eradicate the policies of segregation in Mississippi's dual system of higher education (Gasman, Baez, Drezner & Sedgwick, et. al, 2007).

According to Allen & Jewell (2002), African American student enrollments increased from 83, 000 in 1950 to 666,000 in 1975. However, the biggest differences in enrollments of African – Americans were the type o f institutions in which they were enrolled. In the 1950s most non-white students attended historically black colleges and universities, but by 1975 three quarters of black students attended traditionally white institutions. As reported by Allen & Jewell (2002), more than half a million African Americans had enrolled in college by 1975. This increased the number of Blacks that had some affiliation with a college or university, thus creating a large number of alumni. After so many blacks having received degrees and reaping some of the benefits of the Civil Rights Movement, it would stand to reason that many of these Blacks would contribute to their alma maters. However, according to a study released by the *Journal of Blacks in Higher Education* (2000), many African – American alumni do not give back for a variety of reasons, such as a lack of tradition of higher education philanthropy among black families as compared to white counterparts that have sent generations off to college. Governmental Influences, Philanthropy and Foundations

In considering the history of the various laws that have and will be passed, governmental influences in philanthropy of institutions of higher learning also have come with a price as it pertains to governance. In Smith's (2003) article entitled, *"Governments and Nonprofits"* in the Modern Age, he reveals that many nonprofit agencies are often founded as a result of community interest that seeks to address an issue of mutual concerns. As a first priority, these individuals tend to strive to be responsive to the community, but the government is often motivated by equity concern. Therefore, non profits accepting public funds often have to shift their focus and adopt these governmental priorities. The government still has control or appears to have control over the social issues that can or cannot be addressed and ultimately control how policy and issues will be formulated. This was true even in the colonial era (Cohen, 1998). Smith (2003) also cites that an agency may feel it necessary to change its advocacy with the receipt of public funds. This has and will continue to give governments more control over how programs were operated and funded. Similar to small grassroots organizations of today's time, many of our great universities and colleges were begun because of small groups of people with a common interest. Many of these small groups lacked the expertise to maintain and sustain their organizations through various fund raising efforts, thus creating a need for organizations to seek governmental funding or gifts from foundations or corporations who oftentimes had their own agendas to implement (Smith, 2003).

Turner (2007) states in his article, HBCUs: Making A Case For Support

For the past 18 years, I have taught grant writing courses and emphasized "MACFS" or Making A Case for Support as the most important element of any proposal. This is true of HBCUs as well. Why? The very existence of an HBCU's mission is constantly under review, questioned, or even challenged by those who do not understand their value. Education is a very competitive environment and today African Americans have much broader choices for their educational pursuits than when most HBCUs were established. However, their impact is something that needs to be continually recognized, appreciated and determined. (p. 12).

Turner (2007) goes on to summarize the 2006 National Center for Education Statistics report, "Economic Impact of the Nation's Historically Black Colleges and Universities" by stating that collectively HBCUs' economic impact was over $10 billion dollars and that HBCUs would be listed on the Fortune 500 report ranked 232.

To garner mass support, three philanthropic foundations have cemented a status as strong fundraising entities. They included the United Negro College Fund (UNCF) founded in 1944; the National

Association for Equal Opportunity established in 1969 and the Thurgood Marshall Fund in 1987. Many HBCUs receive or have received funds to support their institutions through scholarships or developmental funds. These foundations have raised billions of dollars for Black colleges. Another notable foundation that has shown substantial support was the Kresge foundation, with its 18 million dollar HBCU initiative in 1999 that supported five HBCUs (Fields, 2001, Powell, 2004, and Schulze, 2005).

One other major governmental boost for HBCUs was the enactment of the White House Initiative for HBCUs. This enactment created several programs that enhanced programs, assisted with enrollment issues and remedial programming (www.ed.gov., 2008).

5 ALUMNI INFLUENCES

The first alumni association was formed at Williams College in 1821. This association came into existence after the administration at Williams College attempted to relocate the school to a new site. Several of the alumni were called together to help intervene and prevent the move (Stover, 1930 as cited in Baker, 2004). Institutions of higher learning have realized that alumni are critical to the continued success of an institution. After the establishment of the first alumni association, many institutions soon followed suit and began incorporating alumni into their institutions by membership on boards of directors and trustees and employing alumni to manage alumni relations and affairs, thus instilling the need for formalized organizations to assist with the financial stability of colleges and universities (Baker, 2004).

Alumni that have vested interests in their alma

maters also may have agendas that they would like instituted at their respective institutions (Cohen, 1998). As the U.S. multiplied, new money became prominent. Families became wealthy, thus increasing the need for more education and more facilities. This newfound wealth made it possible to send more students to college (Cohen, 1998).

Grandillo (1997) argues,

> In order to assure the continuous growth of a community, the Nineteenth century saw development of what is termed *boosterism*. Leaders of a community sought to differentiate and distinguish their town with the mantle of a state capitol, county seat, a right a way of a major road or in the mid-nineteenth century, a railroad. These local leaders, usually landowners themselves, turned to colleges as another economic tool to promote their new towns. Thus the idea of the booster college became established and Ohio provided fertile ground for the movement. (p. 10)

Philanthropic efforts have been around from the beginning of higher educational institutions. Wealthy individuals gave their personal money and or educational artifacts such as books for a library (Cohen, 1998). Hence, many colleges and universities bare the name of benefactors or founders. Private donations may come from alumni, or families of alumni, or foundations such as the Carnegie Foundation. Cohen (1998) notes in his research, that many of the private foundations set up philanthropic foundations as a means of managing the donated funds well before tax laws changed. Philanthropic organizations generally contribute for specific reasons when providing support to higher education institutions, such as research for special need or diverse groups. When organizations accept donated funds, oftentimes, they have to adhere to the concerns and stipulations mandated by the philanthropist. A term used to describe these demands is 'performance philanthropy' (Thurman 2006).

Alumni as philanthropists may deem it necessary to see results or their money at work when making donations. This may come in the form of buildings or rooms being named after them or a new football stadium or the creation of a special endowed chair or scholarship (Cohen, 1998; Thurman 2006). Alumni have and will continue to play a vital role in higher education institutions. From the first graduation of students to become alumni, these individuals were and will continue to be tapped for financial support (Baker, 2004; Ward, 2004).

Student Institutional Involvement

Student involvement at their respective institutions has shown to be a major influence of alumni relationship and involvement post graduation. Previous research has noted that the more involved students were during their matriculation as undergraduates the more likely they were to become donors to their alma maters. Student involvement, whether in an institution sanctioned organization or informal gathering, afforded students the opportunity to build relationships that increase loyalty and commitment to their college or university (Baker, 2004; Hanson, 2000; Ikenberry, 1999).

Tinto (1993) demonstrates in his model on institutional departure that students that are actively engaged academically and socially are more apt to be committed to their institution throughout graduation. The college environment is a web of overlapping interconnected entities that involve both academic and social influences. Students' connection to their institution will often lead to a stronger commitment which in turn leads to more satisfied alumni and an increase in their involvement post graduation (Tinto, 1993).

Tinto (1993) goes on to say that under the integration model there are several phases that include, but are not limited to, the separation phase, a transition phase and an incorporation phase. The incorporation stage is most critical in relationship development. During the incorporation phase a level of commitment and loyalty has become ingrained in the student and has become a part of the student's daily processes and life.

Calvario (1996) adds to this theory by summing up that alumni relationship development begins well before a student graduates. The cultivation of alumni relationships takes a careful and well thought out plan and nurturing while a student is actively engaged on the college campus, which continues post graduation. Student perception of their collegiate customer service and interaction with their campus both academically and socially is an indicator of how students will respond to their alma mater in the future as alumni. Currently enrolled students' needs and satisfaction are imperative to their future involvement with their institution (Baker, 2004; Calvario, 1996).

Volkwein and Parmley's (1999) research noted two attributes of why alumni donors give back to their institutions. They include motivation and capacity. Motivation of alumni to give is affected by the emotional ties to the alumnus' alma mater. Furthermore, positive memories of college life and a desire to see the well being of their institution continue. Secondly, the capacity of alumni's ability to give is based on their socio-economic status. The student's institutional interactions in academic and social settings vary and these interactions play a critical role in the relationship that alumni will have once they graduate from their respective institution. These various interactions and commitments will change over a period of time (Ikenberry, 1999; Volkwein & Parley, 1999).

6 ALTRUISM

One of the main questions that many development and fundraising officials may continuously ask is - how to encourage and increase financial gifts from alumni donors that are consistent and long term. Social learning theorists propose that pro-social behavior (altruism) can be taught or learned and internalized through participation in certain activities and groups as well as through observation (Friedmann, 2003; Mastain, 2007; Morrissey and Werner-Wilson, 2005; Reimer, 2005; Vigoda-Gadot, 2006). Pro-social behavior can be defined for the purpose of this study as alumni giving patterns that are voluntarily given to higher education institutions without the intentions of receiving anything in return. This also defines the altruism of giving by alumni (Friedmann, 2003; Mastain, 2007; Morrissey and Werner-Wilson, 2005; Reimer, 2005; Vigoda-Gadot,

2006).

Scott (2007) defined altruism as giving of time, money and service to others without expecting anything in return. She maintains that this behavior or act is an intrinsic motivator, that is a personal sacrifice albeit financial or physical in nature. Oftentimes this behavior is self-actualized, but it can also be cultivated. Field (2007) emphasizes that altruism or philanthropic behavior can be taught, but it is up to colleges and universities to make sure that they intentionally increase the virtues of philanthropy as well as increase the academic knowledge that is being taught.

Institutional Relations and Socialization

Brown and Davis (2001) propose that Historically Black Colleges and Universities are social agencies and that they enjoyed a unique social contract with Black America. Their dispensation is that HBCUs are the conduits of social capital. Their social contract is at the root of how we think of HBCUs and how these institutions have used their social, political and legal position in higher education to advance African Americans.

Gallo (2003) revealed in his research that alumni who were not satisfied with their institution while enrolled are less likely to become donors upon graduation. If alumni perceive their institution as one of inferior quality, then their financial response will reflect this by a lack of contributions. If students were not socially active during their undergraduate years, they are less likely to become financially active alumni.

Johnson and Eckel (1998) surmised that in cultivating alumni relationships it is hard to rebuild or build good relationships after an alumnus has had a poor collegiate experience or post graduation experience. However, graduates that had positive college experiences are more apt to donate or give of their time to their institutions. Group participation as it pertains to this study is any group or organization sanctioned by the college or university being studied. Group participation addresses an individual or student's participation with a group that encourages and promotes philanthropic activities. The socialization aspect of the individuals' participation in the group promotes identification with the group, thus encouraging philanthropy or volunteerism (Friedmann, 2003; Mastain, 2007; Morrissey and Werner-Wilson, 2005; Reimer, 2005; Vigoda-Gadot, 2006).

Weidman's (1989) sociological aspect of college or institutional relations presents a definition of socialization as being categorized as the inter-active relationships through personal or humanistic contact that conveys the roles and rules of each society. The socialization process continues throughout various phases of a student's or person's life. These phases or roles that a person moves through occur at various points or stages of life as someone transitions into various groups and sub groups particularly as it pertains to college life. Weidman's (1989) model constructs the social process of students' goals that are developed as well as the goals and aspirations that are maintained based on their interaction with an institution of higher learning.

It has been concluded that certain intrinsic and extrinsic motivators encourage or discourage alumni from contributing financially. Development officials attempt to develop marketing based on these motivators in their marketing strategies (Friedmann, 2003; Reimer 2005; Ward, 2004). Extrinsic motivators are generally in the form of gifts, services or public recognition whereas intrinsic motivators are less tangible and persons contribute or volunteer their services because there is a need and the contributor is not looking for anything in return. This motivation embodies the principle of altruism (Baker, 2004; Ward, 2004; Reaves, 2004).

Fund -Raising Principles

Gasman (2001) reported in her historical research on Fisk University's use of a fundraising firm in 1940, noting that negative campaign tactics were used to attract donors from corporations, the community and alumni. This research again focuses on what an institution should do to attract donors post graduation. The research did not address what Fisk should have done to cultivate donors when they were students. Baker (2004) assents that alumni relationships start on the day the student enters the institution. After a student graduates is much too late.

Schulze (2005) posits from the Kresge Foundation Initiative that alumni efforts were not viewed as a priority. Most HBCU alumni efforts were on alumni association activities, which is only a small percentage of the alumni base. Furthermore, many HBCU alumni are discontented with their alma mater because they feel their schools were unresponsive to their needs and lacked consistent communication (Schulze, 2005). Schulze (2005) also recognizes that there must be a paradigm shift in the way HBCUs think and respond to alumni and alumni giving. HBCUs must begin to think of alumni as full stakeholders of the institution.

7 MANAGEMENT AND ALUMNI RELATIONS

Customer Relations Management (CRM)

Bedigian (2006) presents customer relations management as relationship marketing and that it is the leading revenue-generating tool. Her organization, Hezel Associates, reveals that more alumni will return to their alma maters in search of old classmates, career guidance networking and continuing education opportunities. She defines customer relations management as the systematic approach using information and ongoing dialogue to build long lasting and mutually beneficial customer relationship (Bedigian, 2006)

The three basic principles of customer relations management are: (1) It must be embraced by the organization from the top leadership down and must embrace new ways of thinking; and (2) It is data dependent not data driven. Finally, (3) Identify lifetime value driven, life style changes; behavior and customer attitudes. In Customer Relations Management, the ability to gather data about customers, store data in an easily accessible format, analysis and using data to effectively communicate with customers are important (Bedigian, 2006).

Relationship Marketing

Hinde(1995)reported four conditions that establish relationships. First, relationships involve reciprocal exchange between active and interdependent relationship partnership. Second, relationships are purposive, providing meaning to the persons who engage in them. Third, relationships are multi-dimensional, providing a range of possible benefits for their participation. Finally, relationships represent a process that changes and evolves across a series of interactions and in response to changes in the context in which they take place (Hinde, 1995).

Total Quality Management (TQM)

Total quality management can be implemented in modern day higher education institutions. However, it has to be modified to be fully useful, since education is a service industry with no tangible products. Total quality management in education must recognize that they serve multiple consumers (Michael, Sower, Victor & Motwani, 1997). Quality is what the consumers state it is in higher education. If higher education consumers are happy with the particular services provided by learning institutions, then quality is acceptable. Institutions of higher learning must define who their customers are and why (Michael, Sower, Victor & Motwani, 1997). Many colleges and universities that have attempted to use TQM have found it difficult to define their students as customers, simply based on the business principle of the customer is always right (Michael, Sower, Victor & Motwani, 1997). Faculty at these institutions found it difficult to apply and did not want their students to feel like they were paying for grades and services. However, if the principles are applied correctly, then the only outcome that the students or customers want is quality service (Michael, Sower, Victor & Motwani, 1997).

Balderston (1995) posits that quality of institutions of higher education must be viewed in several different ways. The university may be known for its quality based on the notoriety of famous alumnus or even faculty or the size of certain departments such as an extensive library collection. Balderston (1995) also presents that Total Quality Management is mainly concerned with the performance of administrative services and the academic excellence of the institution. However, he believes that the academic sectors have not bought totally into the systematic thinking of this discipline. Balderston (1995) discusses that quality in universities is hard to define as well as measure. He presents the main interest is "global" quality which sets up the "pecking" order of institutions, university operations, analysis of the reputation in markets and quality enhancement measures. In using a global viewpoint of the best colleges and universities, it is generally based on the visibility and the areas of distinction among those institutions.

Although assessment in colleges and universities use grade point averages (GPAs) and comprehensive examinations, the institutions fail to recognize two other areas of importance in determining quality. Those areas are "value added in education and the students' potential to perform creatively in their chosen fields of study. Value added in education applies to the way the institution has contributed to the overall success of student achievement (Balderston, 1995).

Holmes and McElwee (1995) argue that TQM is highly inappropriate in higher education because it limits productivity of individuals and makes the academic arena less professional and more formalized by externally imposed systems and procedures. Holmes and McElwee (1995) posits that TQM is too rigid in higher education settings and forces universities to become more "businesslike". This business precept causes institutions to enforce strategies of hard "Human Resource Management" or

HRM. Hard human resource management views people as resources to control in order to achieve cost effectiveness strategic goals. Soft Human Resource Management views people as resourceful humans who have something to offer and can contribute to the total organization and the development of new ideas (Holmes & McElwee, 1995).

8 ALUMNI PERCEPTIONS

This section presents a conceptual framework which provides an evaluation of HBCU alumni perceptions about their respective alma maters and to advocate the use of customer relations management to increase alumni residual giving. It will involve an investigation of social learning theory of altruism and group or student participation coupled with the principles of customer relations management (CRM) and Total Quality Management (TQM) principles to achieve long term giving, program effectiveness, communication, alumni awareness and marketing. This framework was selected because of the business concept of Return of Customer (ROC). Similar to for –profit businesses, the return on customer or alumni, in the case of institutions of higher learning, is how to monopolize getting alumni to return to their alma maters in ways that are financially beneficial to their respective organization (Bedigian, 2006).

Bedigian (2006) demonstrates a type of conceptual framework in The University of Wisconsin – Madison's logo for the Division of Continuing Studies and the Office of Lifelong Learning, which was developed after the study. The University of Wisconsin – Madison's Office of Alumni Lifelong Learning with a partnership between the Wisconsin Alumni Association and the Division of Continuing Studies developed a goal of offering alumni multiple opportunities of educational and enriching services (Bedigian, 2006).

The Wisconsin Model was able to identify multiple ways for alumni to connect, what they termed as "touching points". Their newly designed logo depicts the inner spokes, similar to a bicycle tire, that touch or affect the student / alumni's needs or services, as well as changing life patterns (Bedigian, 2006). With this concept, they were able to capture and calculate the "Return on Customer" (ROC) principle, which is applied in the business community. Measured in dollars, Return on Customer (ROC) equals a firm's current period cash flow from its customer plus any changes in the underlying customer equity, divided by the total customer equity at the beginning of the period (Peppers & Rogers, 2005, (as Cited in Bedigian, 2006)).

For the purposes of this study, Figure 1 visually connects the conceptual framework of the study. The conceptual framework shows the connection of relationships between development and alumni affairs officers, fund raisers, alumni and students and how that connection is made through alumni relations management. The students' connection to fundraising and alumni affairs is developed through group participation and student involvement that will need to be formally connected through alumni relationship management. Fundraisers and development officials will build upon known extrinsic motivators and encourage intrinsic motivators. Pro-social (altruism) behavior should be increased through active participation in social groups. The researcher gathered data from the various participants that showed emerging themes of connections and motivators or the lack there of.

Figure 1 depicts how students enter their institution of choice and become actively involved with the institution through various activities and communications, as well communication with their school of choice. Upon graduation the graduates flow into the realm of being alumni. This is when most alumni are approached to become a donor. The framework shows that there should be some cultivation of the relationship with the alumnus before donations or the request for donations occurs. Development officials are responsible for donor development, opening the lines of communication and the building of relationships. Potentially, an alumnus will make a donation albeit small or large. Upon the initial donor investment, continuous cultivation must be made with the alumnus. Ultimately, the institution would like for the alumni donor to become a legacy with increased donations and residual giving each year.

Conceptual Framework

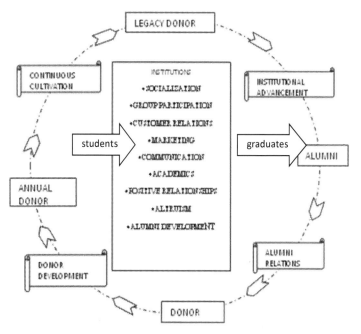

Institutional Alumni Relationship Management Model:

Despite years of turbulent financial crises that have faced many HBCUs, the fact remains that Historically Black Colleges and Universities have maintained a consistent history in American culture of almost 175 years. As HBCUs approach the 200-year mark, they must continue to cement their foothold as viable, meaningful and important educational institutions (Cohen, 1998). As some of the relevant literature has revealed, alumni giving is important. However, HBCUs must seek ways to improve upon this line of financing, as well as develop other meaningful and consistent forms of revenue to firm up their coffers. This study examines ways of cultivating alumni to become long term donors of financial resources to their respective alma maters and factors that may hinder development in this arena.

9 ANALYSIS OF ALUMNI GIVING

This study explored how HBCU alumni relations are cultivated and how this influences alumni giving back to their respective institutions financially. Facilitating a qualitative research analysis of alumni giving was executed according to the following design.

Research Questions

The research questions that guided this study are as follows:

1. What are HBCUs doing to cultivate alumni relationships during the student's undergraduate years to create a feeling of involvement with the university and to become active alumni donors after graduation?

2. What are alumni affairs officers and other fund raising officers doing to encourage individuals or group participation that will enhance alumni giving at HBCUs?
3. What fund raising strategies are HBCUs using to build successful alumni relationships and management systems?

Rationale for Methodology

Phenomenology or phenomenological interviewing was used in this qualitative research study. Marshall and Rossman (2006) define phenomenological interviewing as a means of obtaining grounded themes of lived experiences and how one perceives or interprets those experiences to determine a world view. This method was chosen so that it would allow the researcher the opportunity to obtain detailed descriptions of life events, interactions, direct quotes, thoughts, and lived situations. This is also known as "thick description" (Creswell, 1998, 2003; Marshall & Rossman, 2006). In this study, the researcher attempted to comprehend the phenomena of alumni giving and/ or participating in the development of alumni, particularly alumni of historically black colleges and universities (Denzin & Lincoln, 2007). Marshall and Rossman (2006) state further that in depth interviewing is more conversational and may elicit more information than pre-determined questionnaire type answers. Marshall and Rossman (2006) go on to say that the research population answers may present a more subjective view when the research interview is conducted in this format versus a more triangulation type of data collection.

In framing the theoretical approach, the research explored the principles of etic and emic research when conducting research on Black colleges or persons affiliated with HBCUs (Brown, 2003). Brown (2003) states in his research that emic and etic denote a fundamental distinction of approach, analysis and interpretation of the same thing, event or discourse. Emic research should explore participants of a particular population of research based on their culture beliefs, behaviors, and habits during a specific period or determined accounts of events while under investigation. Etic research should use specific accounts or events that are deemed acceptable by scholarly research principles that are conceptually guided. Emic research is research done on the workings of an internal culture and etic research is external through observations (Brown, 2003).

Assumptions and Biases

The researcher does present some biases. First, the researcher is an alumnus of a comprehensive, public, four-year Historically Black University. Next, the researcher is an active member in said institution's alumni association and has held leadership roles in that association. The researcher will attempt to limit his involvement with current alumni association programs during the research period as well as attempt to limit contact with established or active members of said alumni association. As a secondary mechanism to minimize biases, the researcher kept a reflective journal and used the services of peer reviewer to debrief the study.

Site Selection

After receiving IRB approval (See Appendix A), the researcher interviewed alumni of two historically black colleges and universities. Both of the schools are located in two predominantly, black urban cities located in the southern region of the United States. According to the federal mandate, any institution that seeks to have the distinction of a historically black college or university must have been established or founded prior to1964 (U.S. Department of Education, 2008). Both of the institutions selected meet this mandate. In order to capture data and perceptions of alumni of HBCUs, the researcher chose two HBCUs, one public institution and one private institution. Miles and Huberman (1994) posit that highlights of a case present what is normal, typical and/or average for the entire research population or case. In this research study, the typical aspect is that the alumni of the research sites are predominantly African – American and they attended a historically black college or university.

The first institution, hereafter referred to as Public Comprehensive University (PCU), is a public, four year HBCU located in a state capitol. The metropolitan population of the city where PCU is located is estimated at 200,000. Public Comprehensive University is a comprehensive, research, four-year public university. The student population is currently over 8,000 students.

The second institution will be known hereafter as Private Liberal Institution (PLI). Private Liberal Institution is located in an urban, predominantly African -American city. Private Liberal Institution is a private, 4-year institution. The metropolitan population of the city where PLI is located is estimated at 655,000. The current student population is less than 1,000 students. Both institutions are located in cities that have a large concentration of alumni that graduated from their respective schools.

Participant Selection

Creswell's (2003) principles of simple criterion selection were used to identify potential participants. The criterion sampling seemingly works well, when the individuals to be studied represent who have potentially experienced or are living the phenomenon that is being studied (Creswell, 1998 & 2003). The study explored African American alumni of the two pre-selected schools as the first criterion. The second criterion for participant selection was alumni of the historically black colleges and universities mentioned earlier in the study that matriculated at least 10 years ago or more. Based upon the mentioned criteria, the researcher randomly selected 12 active and / or non-active alumni from the two selected HBCUs. In addition to the 12 alumni selected, 4 alumni affairs and / or development officers were interviewed for the study. The researcher received permission from both alumni affairs directors to gain access to alumni databases for random selection of active and non-active alumni. In order to gain access to alumni, the researcher solicited by mail and followed –up with electronic email contact with the national alumni association and alumni affairs departments (See Appendices B and C). Upon gaining access to the participants, the alumni affairs directors served as the "gatekeepers" (Creswell, 1998).

The researcher had direct access to both active and non active alumni of Public Comprehensive institution (PCU) through participation in the alumni association. The researcher contacted participants via postal mail and electronic mail in order to contact and interview participants (See Appendix D). In order to gain access to alumni of Private Liberal Institution (PLI), the researcher solicited by phone, mail and followed –up with electronic email contact with the alumni affairs officers (See Appendices A and B). The interviewer obtained consent from the interviewees before conducting interviews (See Appendix D) (Creswell, 1998, Marshall & Rossman, 2006).

Data Collection Procedures

The researcher used the interview method to collect data from the selected participants. The interviewer used open – ended questions to elicit detailed responses. (Creswell, 1998, Marshall & Rossman, 2006). The in- depth interview method was used for this research study. According to Marshall and Rossman (1999), in-depth interviewing is equivalent to holding conversations. The researcher or interviewer attempted to expose the participant's views in some general areas or topics but also had respect for how the interviewee responded naturally. An interview guide was used to develop initial conversations; however the researcher asked for elaborations, clarifications and re-stating of questions to draw complete and thorough responses (See Appendix E) (Huberman, 1994; Marshall & Rossman, 1999).

The interviews were tape- recorded with the consent of the participants. The researcher anticipated that the interviews should last a minimum of thirty minutes and no more than one and one half hours.

With the assistance of transcribers, the taped interviews were transcribed verbatim.

Data Analysis

The transcribed interviews were used to categorize and organize emerging themes, thought patterns and keywords or phrases. These themes or similarities from the study were coded. Marshall and Rossman (1999) state that typically the data to be analyzed will fall in to six different categories. These categories include organizing the data, generating categories, themes and patterns, data coding, initial understandings, alternative explanations and report writing.

Trustworthiness

In addressing the credibility of the study, the researcher expressed a trusting explanation of the phenomenon in question by using thick or rich descriptive narrations. As for transferability, the researcher provided, comprehensively, the knowledge of the field work for readers to decide whether the study and the environment in which it was conducted is conclusive and whether the findings can be applied to the similar settings (Creswell, 1998; Marshall & Rossman, 2006; Somekh & Lewin 2005). The researcher explored external audits to validate the study.

In terms of dependability, the researcher attempted to provide information and a context for other researchers to be able to repeat the investigative study by describing the circumstances that are unique to qualitative research (Marshall & Rossman, 2006). For confirmability, the researcher attempted to show that the findings emerged from the participant data that were collected through the interviewing process. The researcher interviewed the participants until the data had saturated (Marshall & Rossman, 2006).

Delimitations

For the purpose of this phenomenological study, the researcher only investigated two historically black colleges and universities, which included one private college and one public university. There are approximately 103 HBCUs in the United States that are either public or private, two or four year institutions. The study geared its focus primarily on alumni and institutional relations at four year institutions.

Limitations

The limitations of the study basically resulted in the limitation of the design and analysis that the researcher utilized with the study. The absence of generalizability from the particular environment of participating research, individuals will be considered as another limitation of the study. In attempts to minimize limitations, the researcher's random selection included active and non-active alumni based on the definitions given in the literature review. Also the selection of a public and a private institution helped with minimization. As a part of the data collection procedures, body language and other natural setting notes were documented during the interviews; however, notations were minimal if interviews were conducted via the phone. The findings for the study were insightful at the least and added to the body of knowledge on alumni relations.

10 EMERGENT THEMES

The purpose of this study was to examine HBCU alumni perceptions about their respective alma maters and how that impacts their giving back to the institution. The data were initially developed into six themes: (1) social learning theory of altruism, (2) student involvement or group participation, (3) customer (alumni) relations management and Total Quality management (TQM), (4) institutional relations and socialization, (5) fundraising and (6) relationship marketing. The creation of these themes is what Marshall and Rossman (1999) describe as analyst-constructed typologies which are based on the gathered data but not necessarily used by the participants in the research study. However, the researcher also used inductive analysis for the discovery of emerging themes and categories (Patton, 2002). After using inductive analysis the following themes emerged from the data: (1) student perceptions of alumni, (2) mentoring, (3) faculty involvement and relationships, and (4) in-kind donations.

Description of Sites

Public Comprehensive University (PCU)

Public Comprehensive University (PCU) founded in 1877 is a public, four year HBCU located in a state capital. The metropolitan population of the city where PCU is located is estimated at 200,000. The city is predominantly African American. Comprehensive University is a comprehensive, research, four-year public university. The student population is currently over 8,000 students. There are a larger number of alumni currently living in the city. PCU offers 39 undergraduate majors and 45 graduate majors. The academic divisions are separated into six colleges: College of Business; College of Education and Human Development; College of Liberal Arts; College of Lifelong Learning; College of Public Service; and the College of Science, Engineering and Technology. In addition to these colleges, the graduate school division is similarly set-up in the aforementioned divisions.

Private Liberal Institution (PLI)

Private Liberal Institution opened in 1871. It is

located in an urban, predominantly African -American city. Private Liberal Institution is a private, 4-year institution. The metropolitan population of the city where PLI is located is estimated at 655,000. The current student population is less than 1,000 students. There is a large concentration of alumni in the city. PLI is a small liberal arts institution. PLI offers 21 areas of study that lead to undergraduate degrees in Bachelor of Science, Bachelor of Arts and Bachelor of Business Administration. The academic programs are divided into five divisions. They are as follows: the Division of Fine Arts and Humanities, Business and Economic Development, Social and Behavioral Sciences, Natural and Mathematical Sciences and Education. PLI offers several activities for their students. The following majors are offered at PLI: Art, major (B.A.) and minor; Biology, major (B.S.) and minor; Business Administration, major (B.B.A.) and minor; Chemistry, major (B.S.) and minor; Computer Science, major (B.S.) and minor; Criminal Justice, interdisciplinary major (B.A.); Early Childhood Education, major (B.S.); English, major (B.A.) and minor; General Mathematics (B.S.) and minor; General Science (B.S.) and minor; History, major (B.A.) and minor; Humanities, interdisciplinary major (B.A.); Language Arts (B.S.); Mathematics, major (B.S.) and minor; Music, major (B.A.) and minor; Political Science (B.A.) and minor; Social Science, interdisciplinary major (B.A.); Social Studies, interdisciplinary major (B.S.) minor; Social Work, major (B.S.); Sociology, major (B.A.) and minor; Special Education (B.S.).

Description of Participants

In order to protect the identities of the research participants, each participant was given a fictitious name. Each participant's year of graduation was used with their fictitious name in order to coincide with the criterion for selection of at least 10 years since their graduation as dictated by the research design mentioned in Chapter 3. Six alumni from Public Comprehensive University and six from Private Liberal Institution were interviewed. Also the researcher interviewed the alumni affairs directors at both institutions as well as one representative from the Development offices at both institutions. Their identities are also protected by the use of fictitious names. A total of 16 interviews were conducted. The following are brief descriptions of the alumni participants in the study.

PCU Alumni:
 Keisha, 1994
 Keisha is a 36 year old, African -American female. She is single and has a 14 year old son. She is a 1994 graduate of PCU. She was active in several student organizations, such as the Student Government

Association, modeling squad, a class officer and a member of the National Association of Black Journalists. Keisha's interview took place at her office. The setting was comfortable and basically a quiet environment. There were not any distractions during the interview. Keisha has been active in the alumni association off and on for the past few years.

Carlos, 1981

Carlos is a 43 year old, African-American male. He is married with three children. He was not active in any student organizations. He was married when he attended PCU. He graduated in 1981. Carlos was very apprehensive at first during his interview. The researcher had to make a few return calls to set-up the interview. Carlos has never been a part of the alumni association nor has he made any financial contributions to PCU. He did not want to meet in person and preferred that I interview him over the phone. Carlos was not the traditional student as an undergraduate. He returned from the military to pursue his degree, and he was married with children when he attended PCU.

Jimmy, 1973

Jimmy is a 60 year old African-American male. He is married with no children. He was a member of the football team and participated in a student Bible study group. He is a 1973 graduate of PCU. Jimmy was a transfer student from another HBCU located in Arkansas. He was dismissed from that institution and came to PCU. Jimmy is an active member of the alumni association and has made some financial contributions to PCU. I interviewed Jimmy at his home.

Doris, 1989

Doris is a 45 year old African-American female. She is married and has two children. Her husband also attended PCU. He is a member of Phi Beta Sigma Fraternity, and she is a member of Zeta Phi Beta Sorority. She was a former president of the Pan-Hellinic council and an honors student. Doris was introduced to her local alumni chapter through a church member that was active at the time. Doris's interview was conducted over the phone.

Loretta, 1983

Loretta is a 48 year old African-American female. She is single with no children. She was active with Delta Sigma Theta Sorority and a member of Delta Mu Delta. She is a 1983 graduate of PCU. She was active with her local alumni association chapter but has not been active for a couple of years now. I interviewed Loretta via the telephone. She was very talkative and provided very good responses.

Tony, 1999

Tony is a 40 year old African-American male. He is single with no children. He was involved with the Political Science club. He graduated in 1999. Tony has never been active financially or through membership in the alumni association. He was very eager to answer the questions of the interview and requested the questions prior to the interview. Tony's interview took place at his office. This was a private office, and we did not encounter any distractions. Tony attended a pre-dominantly white institution prior to attending PCU.

PLI Alumni:

Lisa, 1993

Lisa is a 39 year old African-American female. She is a single mother with two children. She was active with the student government association and a community involvement group. She is a 1993 graduate of PLI. Lisa has not been an active member of the alumni association but expressed that it is time that she become active. I interviewed Lisa at her place of employment. Her office setting was a multi-purpose office and there were people and clients coming and going. It took some time to get the interview started. However, after the initial distractions, the interview continued without any further incidents or distractions.

Nina, 1986

Nina is a 45 year old African -American female with three children. She was a peer counselor and tutor, while a student at PLI. She graduated in 1986. Nina's interview was conducted at her place of employment. She was called into an important meeting right before the interview was scheduled to start. The interview started out somewhat rushed but finally we were able to get settled in to a good pace with the questions and answers. Nina also stated that when she was a student her mother was very sick with cancer and was not able to participate in as many activities as she would have liked too.

Dale, 1994

Dale is a 35 year old African -American male. Dale's interview was conducted at his office. He has been an active alumnus and has made donations to his institution. He is single. He was active with the Student Government Association. He transferred to PLI after being dismissed from a predominantly white institution's football team due to an injury. He pledged Omega Psi Phi Fraternity while at PLI. He was also an honor student. He graduated in 1994.

Rosalyn, 1999

Rosalyn is a 48 year old African- American female. This interview was conducted in the office of the Vice president of Development. It was a great setting.

There were not any distractions during the interview. His office was very well furnished and decorated. Rosalyn was an honor student and a member of a fraternity sweetheart group. Rosalyn returned to PLI after dropping out for a while. She graduated in 1999.

Janice, 1979

Janice is a 52 year old African -American female. She is married with two children. While a student, she was a member of the social work club, the student government association, the yearbook staff and she pledged Delta Sigma Theta Sorority. She is a 1979 graduate of PLI. Janice works for PLI. Her family has a legacy of attending PLI. Her brothers and step brothers attended as well as numerous other family members. She shared that she is trying to recruit her daughter to attend PLI as well.

Robert, 1976

Robert is a 55 year old African -American male. He is a divorced father with three grown children. He pledged Kappa Alpha Psi Fraternity while at PLI. He was active with the student government association and a class president. He graduated in 1976. Robert's interview was conducted at his home. Outside of the occasional phone ringing, the setting was quite natural and pleasant.

Table 2 is a list of alumni demographics by Alumni

Demographics by Name, Graduation Year, Gender, Age and Institution.

Table 2

Alumni Demographics by Name, Graduation Year, Gender, Age and Institution

Name	Graduation Year	Gender	Age	Institution
Dale	1994	Male	35	Private
Janice	1979	Female	52	Private
Lisa	1993	Female	39	Private
Nina	1986	Female	45	Private
Robert	1976	Male	55	Private
Rosalyn	1999	Female	48	Private
Carlos	1981	Male	43	Public
Doris	1989	Female	45	Public
Jimmy	1973	Male	60	Public
Keisha	1994	Female	36	Public
Loretta	1983	Female	48	Public
Tony	1999	Male	40	Public

Alumni Affairs Directors and Development Officers

As a part of the research pool, the alumni affairs directors of both institutions were interviewed as well as development officers. The following is a brief description of those participants.

Alumni Affairs Directors

Maxine, PCU Alumni Affairs Director

Maxine is a 54 year old African -American female and a former student of PCU. She graduated in 1977. She has been employed by PCU as the Alumni Affairs Director since 2004. Maxine's interview was conducted over the phone. She was very cooperative in getting the information to me about the alumni that meet the criterion for random selection process.

Rubbie, PLI Alumni Affairs Director

Rubbie is a 59 year old African-American female. She has worked for PLI for many years but has only been the Director of Alumni Affairs for over a year. She had previously worked in the admissions office. She is also a former student of PLI. She graduated in 1980. Her family has a history of attending PLI. Her sister and a brother each graduated from PLI. Rubbie's interview was conducted in the Alumni Affairs office. They recently underwent an extensive renovation of this historic building. The building that her office is housed in is the former president's campus home.

Development Officers

Lewis, PLI Vice President of Development

Lewis is a 67 year African-American male. He is the vice –president of Development. Although Lewis is not a graduate of PLI, he attended an HBCU as a student. He has been employed at PLI for two months. Most of Lewis's higher education career has been at Pre-dominantly white institutions. Lewis's interview was conducted in his office. His office was nicely furnished and decorated well. There were not any distractions during the interview.

Debra, PCU Development Officer

Debra is a 42 year old African -American female. She is a donor relations specialist at PCU. She has been employed with PCU since 2001. She is also a graduate of PCU. Debra's interview was conducted via the telephone. She was on her way to an appointment and was initially driving. However, she eventually arrived to her appointment and was able to continue the interview. There was noise in the background and sometimes the questions had to be repeated for clarity.

Table 3 depicts the Alumni Affairs and Development Officers by Name, Gender, Age,

Institution and Position. Table 4 shows the total number respondents by Institution and gender.

Table 3

Alumni Affairs and Development Officers by Name, Gender, Age, Institution and Position

Name	Gender	Age	Institution	Position
Lewis	Male	67	Private	Vice President of Development
Rubbie	Female	59	Private	Alumni Affairs Director
Maxine	Female	54	Public	Alumni Affairs Director
Debra	Female	42	Public	Development Officer

In Table 3, the median age for the alumni affairs and development officers is 55.5 years of age. The majority of these respondents were female.

Table 4

Total of Respondents by Institution and Gender

In Table 4, the majority of the respondents were female. The total number of respondents was evenly distributed across both public and private institutions.

Institution	No. of Male Respondents	No. of Female Respondents	Total
Public	03	05	08
Private	03	05	08
	06	10	16

11 ALTRUISM IN EFFECT

Social learning theorists propose that pro-social behavior (altruism) can be taught or learned and internalized through participation in certain activities and groups as well as through observation (Friedmann, 2003; Mastain, 2007; Morrissey and Werner-Wilson, 2005; Reimer, 2005; Vigoda-Gadot, 2006). Scott (2007) defined altruism as giving of time, money and service to others without expecting anything in return. She maintains that this behavior or act is an intrinsic motivator, which is a personal sacrifice albeit financial or physical in nature. Oftentimes this behavior is self-actualized, but it can also be cultivated. If cultivated properly, altruistic behavior can be a guiding force to increased revenue via alumni. One alumnus, Jimmy, recounts how his institution helped him after he left another HBCU, which in turn has caused the premise of altruism to be ingrained in him:

> I was helped by a bunch of people and Coach H. and Coach G. at that time, me and 8 others were helped to get in school. They didn't do anything illegal. They got on us and made us promise to get our lesson this time and gave us a second chance. So, all that stuck with me and I got a second chance. I think everyone needs a second chance in life and if you get a second chance, you need to do the right thing and study your lesson and be the right group. I wasn't a bad guy, but I was just running with the guys that never went to church, and I always went to Sunday school and church...I was with the wrong group. So I turned that thing around and it's just good to help and give back because that's my way of remembering... I was helped and I want to do what I can to help. I always said, I don't know why I waited so late before I got into this... active alumni, but if God let me live I was going to give back something to PCU because PCU helped me. (Jimmy, 1973)

With the close ties that many colleges and

universities have with religious organizations and churches, a sub theme that is ingrained in altruistic behavior is that of church giving or do unto others as you would have them to do unto you or commonly known as the Golden Rule. Loretta 1983 related alumni giving to tithing in the church:

> You know, whether it was an organization or somebody encouraging me to do it from the very beginning, it was hard to do. It's like when you're a member of a church and you don't really know what tithing means; it's like someone has to teach you to do it. It's a hard thing. You know you're supposed to do it. They teach you to do it, and you have to do it a little bit at the time. So then you have to play catch up, as a giving alumnus. You know, you start out giving and then if you don't have the encouragement along the way, you fall by the wayside. And so you don't give as often as you could or as you should and then you may get to a point where you're not giving at all. But if it's something that starts out at the very beginning and it's expected, I think that would get students, getting in the mode to know, okay, when I get out

> of college, get my job, first thing I do is I pay my student loan then I know I need to pay my alumni dues and then I need to give back to the University because I know there are students out there like me who need money and the funding that they're going get from the school is not enough, I need to help them like I was helped. (Loretta, 1983)

Student Involvement

As reported earlier in the study, the literature revealed that students who were involved in student activities or organizations tend to be more acquainted with alumni affairs or contributors to their institutions post graduation. Tinto (1993) refers to this in his integration model. In Tinto's integration model, during the incorporation phase is when institutional commitment and loyalty are most prevalent. Calvario (1996) surmised that alumni relationship cultivation begins well before the student graduates.

Of the 12 alumni that were interviewed for this study, 11 of the participants reported being very active as students. The alumni participants participated in everything from peer counselors and tutors to student government associations and sororities and fraternities. Both alumni affairs directors and two development officers were interviewed for the study. Each of these staff members mentioned the pre-alumni clubs at their institutions during their interviews as means of student involvement. Nine of the twelve alumni participants mentioned the pre-alumni club and neither one of them was a member of the organization.

Private Liberal Institution (PLI) Alumni Affairs Director, Rubbie states:

> When the students are here we have several organizations, but the organizations- student organizations pre alumni club is the club that we allow students to participate while they're here. And they can join the uh pre alumni club when they are freshmen. They do not have to have a defined major. They uh have to uh have uh to indicate some type of leadership skill. (Rubbie, PLI Alumni Affairs Director)

Maxine, PCU Alumni Affairs Director:

> Okay, well one of the methods is that within my office (the office of alumni and constituentsf relations) we have uh, the advisor here, who is one of my staff persons. And he is the advisor of the

pre alumni club. The pre alumni club is composed of students, primarily who reside here in PCU. But we also have other students who are in other state clubs at the University like the Illinois club, the Tennessee club, the Texas club…and those clubs encourage um, camaraderie with other persons in your area to make you feel more comfortable while you're here at PCU particularly for freshmen… that's very important. But the pre alumni club also allows students the opportunity to learn early all about the importance of giving back to the University. We have these students to help with various events of the national alumni association and they also volunteer for the office of development for various functions. So, yes…we do include them, I think we should do more… (Maxine, PCU Alumni Affairs Director)

Loretta:

Good question, I'll be honest with you, I didn't have… I knew of what's known as the pre alumni club or pre alumni association, knew of it, knew its activities but no one really approached/

encouraged me to join. And I think it was through that organization that a lot of activities and things like what your responsibilities were told to us as to encourage us to be active after we leave. Obviously we saw people being active and by their example we were, it was given to us to be an example, but nobody really, from an official prospective, came and approached me and said hey, "you know, this is an education you're getting here and it doesn't stop there, you need to help the other people, uh, other students that's coming behind you to get involved to give back in terms of finances, and also in terms of the times. (Loretta, 1983)

Similarly, Lewis, Vice-president of Institutional Development at PLI states:

Well we have a director of alumni affairs that works very closely with the president and the national president of the alumni association. They encourage students from time to time. They have pre alumni chapter where they talk to the undergraduates expressing the importance of a continued relationship with the college. During the graduation

> ceremony there is a portion where the president inducts them into the alum association. (Lewis, PLI, Vice President of Development)

PLI alumnus, Janice relays information about the pre-alumni club at her institution:

> I think one of the organizations that we have, and I don't know if you're aware; the pre alumni council. That's a start. For those students who are participants in the pre alumni, we have different activities and different organizations have fund raisers. (Janice, 1979)

One of the notable themes established from the student involvement questions of the research was that some of the organizations that were mentioned had fundraisers for their respective fraternities or sororities and so forth. However their fundraisers were not geared toward support of the institution. Many of the Fraternities and sororities are required to do community service as well as have pledges have some form of community service before being inducted (Brown, 2003). Following are some of the responses that support this aspect of the research:

Janice:
> The Alpha Phi Alpha Fraternity just had

> a fund raiser called the Black and Gold pageant, where the participants had to raise money with a specific goal. A portion of their funds went to the school and part of it went back to the fraternity. The Delta's do the same thing; Delta Sigma Theta has the peppermint pageant and the students have to raise so much money. So a lot of our students are already actively involved in fund raising.

(Janice, 1979)

Loretta tries to recollect her involvement as a student being involved in fundraising activities:

> I don't recall getting involved in anything having to do with fund raising that would help the institution. Um, in fact... I think my prospective back then was that all monies that was given to the school came from wealthy alumni or from the State. Um, I do recall seeing some uh, I guess it was... you have the (Letter) club and different levels I guess of people who had contributed. But, I did not participate in anything to assist the University in terms of raising funds as a student. (Loretta, 1983)

Robert also did not recall ever being involved in fundraiser for his institution:

> Well, at that time, there wasn't anything going on about fund raising at the time I was there.
> Researcher: Okay, so you all did not do anything on the side? What about your fraternity or anything like that? Nothing. (Robert, 1976)

Doris recalls how she was involved with fundraising with her sorority but does not recall being involved with her institutions fundraising activities:

> Well, actually the institution itself did not involve me but being a part of Zeta Phi Beta sorority incorporated, we would do fund raisers um, to help fund programs where we would go to the nursing homes and be able to take fruit and then go to the children's' hospitals and you know, do things as a sorority to help our community.
> Researcher: Okay, did any of the funds that you all raised that, did any of those funds go to the institution or was that just for the sorority?
> Doris: Basically it was for the sorority. I don't remember ever having a fundraiser with the institution the years that I was there to help support the University, no. (Doris, 1989)

12 RELATIONS AND SOCIALIZATION

All of the participants in the study relatively had positive perceptions and feelings toward their alma mater. The respondents of study either reported things about other students that they had knowledge of problems or situations before graduating or while trying to complete graduation requirements. One respondent in the study reported having a problem when she was trying to graduate due to a graduation requirement that was over looked. As far as the impact on alumni giving based on institutional relations, one participant reported that she felt alumni and or students were leery in giving back because of an investigation of mis-appropriation of funds, while she was a student. Overall the respondents in the research believed in their institution and were please with how they were treated during their undergraduate experience. The aforementioned themes are reflected in the respondents' reflections;

Carlos:
> Well, I don't know. I saw a few students that had financial problems um and it seemed to me that the university was primarily interested in getting the tuition money. And um, I thought maybe they could be treated a little bit different some kinda way... I don't know cause I had the G.I. bill to go on so I had no problems there. (Carlos, 1981)

Out of all alumni interviewed only one alumna, Nina, stated that she felt like to had been treated unkindly:
> When I attended PLI, I got a four year scholarship to attend. But during, you know the summer... the scholarship didn't take for the summer time so I needed assistance to continue to get through the summer because I graduated in exactly four years. So in that process I had to get a student loan. So, I got a student loan, I was paying it back, but, I think I had a fine... it was some kind of way I had something I owed anyway, what turned me off personally, was that they went into my account and put a hold on my account and that's how I was like...oh no, this is ridiculous, because I was still a student ...to me they didn't explain further how I needed

> to handle my bill. You know what I'm saying I was thinking I had so many days to do it or months but it just completely turned me off. (Nina, 1986)

Lisa speaks to how a financial situation involving her institution caused her to have reservations about giving back:

> I was not encouraged because while I was attending there, It was a big investigation with our financial representatives it was later learned that they were pocketing some of the money for the uh, as a return of money from the schooling… Pell grants and work study so I was a little hesitant about giving money back. (Lisa, 1993).

Dale:
> Definitely, Um, I was treated with kindness; I was treated with respect and as far as the financial aspect um when I made a payment on books or whatever it was I received a receipt. They kept a record and I kept a record, we did everything as professionals… everything was current, everything was courteous. (Dale, 1994)

Tony:

> I definitely think that the treatment I received as an undergraduate had an impact upon my giving back. Sometimes when I might be tempted to give, I am reminded of college employees who were not so friendly. I also found it very difficult to get a job after graduation at the university. Sometimes I felt that all my tuition money had "gone up in smoke." My college definitely can improve in this area. They have to remember that the student is both their "product and outcome." The students may internalize and remember bad experiences. Treating a student well might result in more alumni giving. (Tony, 1999)

From the perspective of alumni affairs and development officials, they presented relationship building and cultivation at their institution as sound devices for student socialization and interaction.

Lewis:
> I think they can get involved in the pre-alumni association. Uh the main thing and then also they can develop relationships with the admissions office, the recruiting office so when they get out I think they can be those students can be the biggest and best sales person for any institution. When you

> have gone there … there you can appreciate the education you got there. You are the best source to go out and to help recruit those individuals. They can work with the admission office the recruitment office and volunteer to go out to a high school and talk to students try to encourage them to come to their alma mater. (Lewis, PLI, Vice President of Development)

Maxine:
> Okay, well one of the methods is that within my office, we have the advisor here, who is one of my staff persons. And he is the advisor of the pre alumni club. The pre alumni club is composed of students, primarily who reside here in PCU. But we also have other students who are in other state clubs at the University like the Illinois club, the Tennessee club, the Texas club. Those clubs encourage um, camaraderie with other persons in your area to make you feel more comfortable while you're here at PCU particularly for freshmen. That's very important. (Maxine, PCU Alumni Affairs Director).

Customer Relations Management and Marketing

Customer (Alumni) Relations management has

been defined in this study as the reciprocal and purposeful relationship of alumni and institutions of higher learning. It is a systematic use of information and marketing that builds residual and beneficial relationships. Over the course of the interview process, all of the study participants reported that they had good communication with their institution. This communication and marketing was typically done through letters, local alumni chapters, emails and newsletters or magazines. All of the alumni affairs directors and the development officials agreed that the communication could be better. However they felt like the institution did have some financial restraints in marketing information to their constituents.

In analyzing the data of the component of relationship building and cultivating alumni, there were mixed perceptions of what the alumni felt their institutions did to cultivate them to become financially active versus how institutional alumni affairs and development staff felt they developed these relationships. The alumni participants in the study reported they were introduced during their freshman year, but believed it was not really encouraged anymore until the graduation ceremonies by taking the oath to become active alumni. The following responses reflect this theme:

Tony:

>As freshmen, we took a freshman class type

of seminar class. It was mandatory for all freshmen, and we were encouraged to participate in fundraising type of activities with benefactors. Some students who were in the concert choir would travel nationwide and sing at donor events. Some other students who were not as musically inclined participated in other fundraising activities: where we would interact with board members and community leaders. (Tony, 1999)

Dale:
And upon graduation my particular class took an oath. The oath was presented by the President and we took a oath to be a part of Alumni and support PLI. (Dale, 1994)

From the perspective of Alumni Affairs Directors and Development staff, they promoted their students programs and organizations as the method of building relationships. But reportedly, some of the communication was viewed as poor relationship development such as the first contact was a solicitation for money through form letters.

Debra:
Because what we tend to do is approach our alumni with all of these appeals letters and

phone calls soliciting funds and a lot people feel that they have not really reached out to me and that is true and we are not really reaching out to those that need to be reached out and those are the people that they really need to be reached. I think those are the alumni that are not paid alumni in the alumni association. In the future what we need to work on is more personalized communication with the alumni. I personally think of email. (Debra, PCU staff)

Table 5 demonstrates alumni perceptions of communication with their institutions. The first column shows the respondents of the study, which includes alumni, alumni affairs directors, and development officers. The second column depicts the type of communication the alumni received or what was delivered by institutional staff. In third column it shows perception of how frequently alumni received these various types of communication.

Table 5

Alumni Perceptions of Institutional Communication

Respondents	Type of Communication	Frequency of Communication
Alumni	Email	Often
	Local Chapters	Often
	Form Letters	Periodically
	Newsletters / Magazines	Rarely
	Internet	Periodically
Alumni Affairs Directors	Email	Often
	Local Chapters	Often
	Mailings	Frequently
	Newsletters	Periodically
Development Officers	Emails	Often
	Internet	Often
	Letters	Often

Relationship Marketing

Marketing strategies, participation, and support of the alumni were very similar at both institutions. The alumni periodically received letters, emails, Facebook messages or newsletter type communications. It was apparent that the alumni and the staff at both institutions believed they received information consistently, but it could be improved. The pre-alumni clubs were active at both institutions, but many of the respondents did not feel that they were well informed of the purpose of the organization or that they were strongly encouraged to participate. Public Comprehensive University has developed a program for young alumni to get better acquainted with the giving process, through its 24/7 program where young alumni can begin a giving process with as little as $12.00 dollars annually. The following responses discuss marketing strategies.

Debra:
> To be honest our students have not been really involved in fundraising. Because we have not really had to rely on the students, but now, because of the economy; they are cutting our budgets so fundraising is so very important to us. So what we are doing now we have club 24/7. That is specifically geared towards students. And they are able to

continue to let me say graduating students. And they are able to contribute $247 for 5 years. The next year after they graduate they can contribute $12 and so forth. It is a program that is geared to get the students familiar with what fundraising and how important it is. (Debra, CU Development Officer)

The principle of marketing the purpose of alumni to students throughout their tenure as students more consistently and intentionally manifested itself. It was also reported that possibly their institution could develop some type of tracking program. This practice could track the students throughout their experience, in somewhat of an exit interview type program for academic level and for students upon graduating, similar to the way you exit a job. This theme will be discussed further as an implication for practice and policy in chapter Five. This is further demonstrated from the graduates through the following responses.

Rosalyn:
> So, I think if we can do more of that tracking the students from beginning to end and making sure that we have an open door policy, where they can come and talk to anyone about a problem and we can get them

to that right person to work them through that problem. I think would be a good thing. (Rosalyn, 1999)

Keisha:
As I said I had no real input with alumni affairs, we knew that was the alumni affairs building and that was the extent of it. I think they should really infiltrate that into undergraduates to um, to get them started. And not just have a few kids to do it. Ones that may have to work there for work study and things like that. So, I think the alumni experience should start earlier. (Keisha, 1994)

Tony:
Sometimes, I think that my university sometimes only wants to work with the "best of the best" students. It builds relationships with students by encouraging them to be visible during campus sponsored events. I think that alumni giving should be instilled from the freshman experience through their senior year. Every student should want to give. (Tony, 1999)

Alumni Affairs and development officials also agreed that their departments needed to market their programs much sooner and throughout the undergraduate experience.

Debra:
> Well I would have to say that is another area that we are not strong in. We don't have a lot of programs that connect the two together students and alumni. The alumni affairs are doing a little bit with the pre alumni club. They think that you are automatically a part of the pre-alumni. But a lot people want to know the relevance of the club. Our national alumni need to be more visible and hosting more events with the students. In the past, we did workshops with the alumni. We need to show them how the alumni association can benefit them in the future. We really don't do a whole lot. (Debra, PCU development staff)

Maxine:
> I think it starts with student life. I think when the students come in as Freshmen, it's my understanding that during orientation, there is a presentation that is given by the office of development on how to give to CU as an undergraduate student, so when they leave…the office of alumni affairs will continue to remain connected to the student or encourage them to stay connected to the University so they will continue giving.

(Maxine, PCU Alumni Affairs Directors)

Table 6 shows the alumni perceptions of pre-alumni and their institution's ways of building relationships.

Column (A) shows the respondents.

Column (B) shows the alumni's response.

Column (C) shows the perception the response suggests.

It appears that all of the respondents, alumni, alumni affairs directors, and development officers mentioned pre-alumni clubs at their institution. This is reflected in the table. Notwithstanding, the alumni mentioned were not involved as students; however, each of the alumni affairs directors and development officers described this as a good form of building students' knowledge of alumni.

Table 6
Perceptions of Institutional Organizations

Respondents	Source of Alumni Information	Knowledge and Involvement
Alumni	Pre-Alumni Clubs	Knowledge of clubs but not involved
	State Clubs	Knowledge of clubs but not involved
	Alumni Association	Somewhere to socialize after graduation
Alumni Affairs Directors	Pre-Alumni clubs	Promoted to students during Freshmen orientation
	State clubs	Promoted to students
	Alumni Association	Encouraged students join/ Oath at graduation
	24/ 7 club	Opportunity for students to start giving
Development Officers	Pre-Alumni clubs	Promoted to students during Freshmen orientation
	Alumni Association	Encouraged students join/ Oath at graduation
	24/ 7 Club	Opportunity for students to start giving

13 FUNDRAISING AND ALUMNI GIVING

In 1944, a mass support of private HBCUs was established – the United Negro College fund. UNCF and their trademark slogan, "A mind is a terrible thing to waste!" are internationally known and have cemented its stamp as leader in fundraising for private HBCUs. Supporting public HBCUs is the National Association for Equal Opportunity established in 1969 and the Thurgood Marshall Fund founded in 1987. The newest member of HBCU fundraising organizations is the Tom Joyner Foundation with their monthly support of a different HBCU.

Throughout the interviews with alumni from PLI, references were made to the United Negro College Fund (UNCF). In contrast, this was not the case with the alumni from PCU. It also was not apparent that alumni of Public Comprehensive University were aware of the other foundations as mass supporters with various capitol campaigns, nor were the alumni of PCU involved as students in the fundraising efforts of their respective institution. It is apparent from the responses of PI alumni that they each had an opportunity to help raise funds while they were students.

Janice:
> Well, they would have Miss. UNCF at that particular time when I was in school you had to raise so much money to win Miss. UNCF and even though there were young ladies running t from different organizations, we supported everybody…we would sell cookies, we would sell pickles, whatever we could do to help the individual raise money, and I think that helped as I matured to give back to my school. (Janice, 1979)

Lisa:
> We did, each year they had a… there was a marathon Lou Rawl's marathon for Historical Black Colleges and it would be a big rally and we would have uh, have an opportunity to answer the phones and we would have celebrities come to the campus. (Lisa, 1993)

In-kind Fundraising

A secondary fundraising aspect that is oftentimes not calculated properly or financially is in-kind donations. In-kind donations are more than just goods or products given to institutions. This is the volunteer time that an individual or organization dedicates to helping institutions. This developing theme emerged as one that will need more research or study as to the value placed on these services.

Lewis:

> I think they can get involved in the pre-alumni association. Uh the main thing and then also they can develop relationships with the admissions office, the recruiting office so when they get out I think they can be those students can be the biggest and best sales person for any institution. When you have gone there ... there you can appreciate the education you got there. You are the best source to go out and to help recruit those individuals. They can work with the admission office the recruitment office, and volunteer to go out to a high school and talk to students try to encourage them to come to their alma mater. (Lewis, PLI Development Officer)

Debra:
> I think that alumni and development go hand and hand. We rely on them for all kinds of support volunteering and that both offices work together. They may not be able to give. But they can volunteer and do others things to help the alumni association and the development. (Debra, PCU Development Specialist)

Janice:
> If you don't have money, come over here and just volunteer… give in kind. Come and help her down in the alumni office with mailings and typing and recordings, you know, giving and that kind of thing. We have alum right now that's working on the lawn he's coming over, he's retired. He comes over and he helps the crew, to mow, mow the lawn, put the mulch down… I mean he really has been helping. And if we can get more alums to think like that, cause you might not be able to give money, but if you give your time and service to help, the office of institution advancement can record that- that we had twelve thousand alums or we had eight hundred alums who gave in kind and this is an in kind and this is what it equaled up to. (Janice, 1979)

Maxine:

> It's more than just the money, um; when you give you can give your time. You can mentor to students here. We have alumni who are alumni who are millionaires okay? We have alumni who are doing fantastic things in their careers, uh, really ground breakers in every way, all over the world. And these alumni have the capability of giving back to the University because of what they're doing in their careers: Coming in and talking to the students in the classroom sharing information on how to get to where they are. Students are interested in talking to alumni because alumni are where they want to go. So, not only money, money is very important you can never underestimate the importance of money and the financial support that the institution needs. But it's always important to give back emotionally through mentoring, through participation, through partnerships; I think that's very important (Maxine, PCU Alumni Affairs Director).

The Financial Accounting Standards Board (FASB) states that the value of volunteer services whether that is time or product can be included on financial statements for internal and external use. The value of volunteer time can also be used for grant proposals and annual reports. The rule of thumb for using these numbers is what the institution would have had to pay for these services or goods (FASB, 2009).

Table 7 depicts the value of volunteer time per hour, according to Independent Sector (2008).

Table 7
Dollar Value of a Volunteer Hour

Dollar Value of a Volunteer Hour: 1980 - 2007					
1981:	$8.12	**1990:**	$11.41	**2000:**	$15.68
1982:	$8.60	**1991:**	$11.76	**2001:**	$16.27
1983:	$8.98	**1992:**	$12.05	**2002:**	$16.74
1984:	$9.32	**1993:**	$12.35	**2003:**	$17.19
1985:	$9.60	**1994:**	$12.68	**2004:**	$17.55
1986:	$9.81	**1995:**	$13.05	**2005:**	$18.04
1987:	$10.06	**1996:**	$13.47	**2006:**	$18.77
1988:	$10.39	**1997:**	$13.99	**2007:**	$19.51
1989:	$10.82	**1998:**	$14.56	**2008:**	$20.25
		1999:	$15.09		

Note. From

www.independentSector.org/programs/research/volunteer_time.html

Faculty as Mentors and Fundraisers

Throughout the research, the participants referred back to specific faculty members or staff that mentored them while they were students. Reference was given that these individuals influenced them enough while they were students to make them want to give back to their institution in some form or fashion. Inference was also made alumni that could give donations through in-kind services such as by tutoring or mentoring students in the event that they (alumni) are unable to give monetary donations. This emergent theme, although not readily a part of the original framework for the study, presented itself and will be discussed further in Chapter 5. Supporting this theme are some of the responses of the respondents:

Janice:

> Well I had a very good mentor, as a matter of fact, she's still here at PLI, her name is Sheila Hilton. And, uh at that particular time, Ms. Hilton worked in Cooperative Education. She was a very strong influence because she was a Tennessee State graduate but she always encouraged me to be a leader. To get involved in activities on campus and to, be active. Just to be active in what activity whatever was going on to make sure I participated, I attended or whatever. That gave, and plus

freshman orientation. (Janice, 1979)

Dale:

> Yeah, because learning comes from more than our future, it is in our past. There are aspects from my past that I didn't know about and never would have known about if it hadn't been for PLI. And I learned it from actually from Dr. Randolph Walker. He's a professor; well he's probably retired now. (Dale, 1994)

Doris:

> Dr. Harvey was a prime example. When I was there, with the honor students… everybody knew that she checked on her students, you see what I'm saying? Some departments don't check on their students they don't care, you know… basically, it's just pay your dues, but it's more than just paying your fees to go to the University. And I think that the Alumni need to recognize. They can't take for granted that just because somebody gives this time, it is not certain that they are going get that same support next time if they don't stay in touch and show some type of appreciation if no more than a thank you letter or a little card or something remembering them. (Doris, 1989)

Jimmy:
> It's a man, can't think of his name now, I think it was Mr. Johnson, I'm not sure. Mr. Johnson, he was an elderly man they used to have a Bible class on Wednesday nights. We would go over there to Bible class on the side of Penguin's there were real houses right there on the side of Penguin's and he lived over there and he had a rooming house also. And we would go over there and kind of read and study the bible and that kind of a thing. Uh, just off the top of my head right now, I can't think of any other (Jimmy, 1973)

Rosalyn:
> I think probably if we had a mentor program in place actually training with the students actually training them early on when they get here. But it is so many ways that you can give back, maybe you can't do it financially, maybe you can be a tutor or mentor to a student here at the college. (Rosalyn, 1999)

From the aforementioned responses, it was concluded that many of the alumni mentioned faculty and other staff members by name. The respondents remembered coaches, honors directors, professors or department chairs that helped them to matriculate throughout their undergraduate years. It may be concluded that faculty and staff may not be used in the fundraising efforts of their respective institutions that will be financially beneficial.

Perceptions of Alumni and Alumni Association

One of the emerging themes of the research was perception of alumni and or the alumni association. Reportedly, the alumni and the association were viewed as a social organization or "just something you did after graduation" (Keisha, 1994). It is also documented that while they were students, particularly at Public Comprehensive University, that they did not know all of the functions of the alumni such as providing scholarships from local alumni chapters and service activities. The graduates found out more about the alumni association after they graduated.

Keisha:

> I was not. I would say that I was not. Alumni affairs to me and I think to a lot of the people that I was in school with at the time, it was kind of "oh that's what you do when you graduate"… It wasn't, um, really… We weren't put in a position to really understand you know, the way that it was positioned, it was kind of okay when you graduate, you know, then, Alumni affairs will become something that you would be involved in…If

that makes any sense. (Keisha, 1994)

Doris, 1989:
> I didn't even know what the alumni did when I came to PCU, it was after I graduated that I knew that they gave scholarships… I didn't even know that when I was in school that I might could have went to the alumni to get a book award or something like that for help. So, I think they need to get more information to the students so that the students can use all the resources out there. Some people just think the alumni association is just a social club, to fellowship. I mean, that's part of it too, but we do more than just that. It's a perception that people have. (Doris, 1989)

The analyst-constructed typologies originally presented as the conceptual framework for the study have been examined. The data were first grouped into five categories that addressed the research questions. Four emergent themes are also presented that were inductively presented based on the participants' responses throughout the interview process. After considerable coding and in depth data analysis, seven themes are prevalent: (1) social learning theory of altruism, (2) student involvement or group participation, (3) Institutional relations and socialization, (4) customer (alumni) relations management and marketing, (5) Fundraising principles, (6) student perceptions of alumni (7) Faculty involvement and mentoring. The purpose of the study was to determine if HBCU's are cultivating potential alumni relationships through altruistic behavior.

The data revealed that although the institutions are proactive initially in promoting alumni through pre-alumni groups, many of the respondents did not feel any connection to the group or they viewed it as something that you did upon graduation. It is evident that there is a need for extended promotion of alumni affairs and the purpose of giving back to ones respective institution post graduation. Some of the salient factors presented were the opportunity for alumni to get involved through in-kind donations such as volunteering more frequently, become mentors or just be more visible with students.

From the aspect of customer or alumni relations, there appears to be opportunities for development in the communication given to alumni, such as a more deliberate cultivation of alumni before a solicitation for money is made. Also addressing the opportunity for other fundraising principles is the effects of faculty on students. It is presented that faculty are one of the more influential bodies on students, thus having a bigger impact on the connection students have with their institution.

In addressing the effects of the social learning

theory of altruism, which is the giving of an individual's time and money without expecting anything in return, alumni and alumni affairs/development officials are in agreement that HBCUs present an environment that is conducive for social behavior; however, it does not always reflect in the monetary aspect of giving back to their institution particularly as it pertains to HBCUs.

14 DISCUSSION AND CONCLUSIONS

This chapter examines the study's findings and draws conclusions that will inform policy and practice as well as delve into topics of future research. The revelation from the participant interviews has presented insight into the cultivation and management of alumni as donors at Historically Black Colleges and Universities. The conceptual framework tenets of the study were predisposed through the interview questions; howbeit the emergent themes added credence to the typologies of institutional relations and the perception of impact on alumni giving, as it pertains to HBCUs.

Under the disposition of the social learning theory of altruism, which is the giving back of time, service and finances without expecting anything in return, this section addresses the phenomenon of alumni giving at HBCUs. It has been well documented that the rate of giving at HBCUs is at a dismal level as compared to predominately white institutions (CAE, 2008; US News & World Report, 2008). The other salient influences and findings, such as student involvement, institutional relations and socialization, customer relations and total quality management and fundraising principles are discussed throughout this chapter. Finally, this chapter presents the need for further research in the areas of student perceptions of alumni at HBCUs, faculty as fundraisers, mentoring programs, the tracking and importance of in kind donations and the effectiveness of pre-alumni associations at HBCUs.

Overview of Study

The purpose of this study was to address to what extent HBCUs are cultivating alumni relationships by promoting altruistic behavior in student involvement, institutional relations, socialization, customer relations, and fundraising principles. Furthermore, the study sought to find out how these salient themes impacted alumni giving at Historically Black Colleges and Universities.

The extant literature review has revealed that most studies on alumni giving are monolithic and one-sided focusing on factors that influence or deter alumni giving. Some of those factors include socio-economic status, race, gender, time since graduation or comparison studies of predominately white institutions and historically black institutions (Baker, 2003, Hunter, 1999, Ward, 2004). Few empirical studies have focused on the dichotomous relationship building efforts between institutions and alumni donors (Freidmann, 2003).

Friedmann (2003) documented Schverish's (1993) study on communities of participation and socialization and how student involvement while attending impacted alumni giving through student participation in the identified organizations of student foundations or student alumni groups. The main concept of these studies was on the social learning theory of pro-social behavior also known as altruism and how this influences alumni giving post graduation.

The research questions that guided this study included:

1. What are HBCUs doing to cultivate alumni relationships during the student's undergraduate years to create a feeling of involvement with the university to become active alumni donors after graduation?
2. What are alumni officers or fund raising officials doing to encourage student or group participation that will enhance alumni giving at HBCUs?

3. What fund raising strategies are HBCUs using to build successful alumni relationships and management systems?

The data gleaned from the interview construction is developed into eight themes: (1) social learning theory of altruism, (2) student involvement or group participation, (3) Institutional relations and socialization, (4) customer (alumni) relations management and marketing, (5) Fundraising principles, (6) student perceptions of alumni (7) Faculty involvement and mentoring and (8) in-kind (volunteer hours) donation programs.

Research Question #1

The first research question that guided the study dealt with the theme - student involvement or group participation and the social learning theory of altruism. The majority of alumni respondents of the research study each expressed some type of student involvement with their institution. They reported participation in peer counseling groups, student government associations, sororities and fraternities to name a few. The alumni affairs directors and development officials each reported on the pre-alumni associations at their respective institutions and often referenced this as a point of contact for the initial introduction to the premise of alumni giving. However, none of the alumni reported being active members of this association, while they were students. The other groups or organizations that the participants were a part of each did fundraising for the group that they belonged to but did not recall any of the funds going to the institutions. Only one respondent reported having raised funds for their institution through their social groups. As far as student participation in fundraising on a consistent basis, this was proven through the alumni at Private Liberal Institution (PLI). Each of the PLI respondents reported having knowledge or participating in fundraising activities for United Negro College Fund (UNCF).

With the evidence of student involvement in groups and activities of the alumni participants, Tinto's (1993) integration model is applicable here. It appears that the alumni were active in many diverse organizations to help facilitate the incorporation phase of loyalty to their institution and or student groups that were associated with their institution. Tinto (1993) presents in integration model the phase of incorporation. The incorporation phase is when students develop a sense of loyalty and commitment to their respective institution and makes it a part of their daily life processes.

Altruism

In applying the socialization theory of altruism, it

is evident that alumni that attended historically black institutions have a sense of family and pride for their college. Many of the respondents stated that they loved their school and wanted to see great things happen. Nevertheless, this was not evident in their active status of giving back consistently to the institution. Altruism is defined as doing something for someone or something and not expecting to receive anything in return (Scott, 2007). Many of the respondents reported not being approached enough about giving back to their institution while they were students. The alumni reported vaguely having knowledge of the pre-alumni associations and that they recall very few intentional requests to give throughout their tenure as students. Schervish (1993) and Friedmann (2003) each posits that altruism or pro-social behavior can be cultivated or taught, if it is not already a part of a person's psychological make-up.

Research Question #2

The second research question that guided the study reflected on what are alumni or development officials doing at their institutions to encourage student participation that will enhance alumni giving. The themes that reflect on this question include: Institutional relations and socialization, customer (alumni) relations management and marketing.

Gallo (2003) surmised that if alumni were not satisfied with their undergraduate experience then they are less likely to become active donors post graduation. Johnson and Eckel (1998) go on to say that in cultivating alumni relationships it is hard to build or re-build good relationships after an alumnus has had a poor collegiate experience. Most of the respondents reported having a good collegiate experience. One respondent reported a poor customer service experience that initially turned her off about her institution but having family members that attended and worked for the institution has changed how she thinks about the institution.

As far as marketing to alumni, the respondents felt that they received adequate communication but believed some areas could be improved upon such as the frequency of distribution and the manner of distribution (i. e. emails, newsletters, magazines). The institutional staff from both institutions also believed that communications could be better but they were limited to the type of hard communication (i.e. publications) that they are able to produce due to budget constraints. One development staff person reported that she did not necessarily believe in the form letter type of solicitation because it did not embody cultivation of the alumnus.

Research Question #3

The third research question examines what fundraising strategies are HBCUs using to build successful alumni relationships and management systems? The principles of fundraising were the themes that addressed this point of the study. The alumni in the study each discussed some connection with fundraising from their institution. The strongest fundraising involvement with students and what some alumni remember was the United Negro College Fund. This was evident with the alumni of PLI. Each of the respondents from PLI mentioned UNCF. In contrast, the alumni from PCU did not mention any national body that was a consistent funding source or fundraiser across the board for public colleges and universities. We do know from the literature that there are other national organizations such as the Thurgood Marshall Fund, NAFEO and the Tom Joyner Foundation that raise money and provide services to assist public colleges and universities as well (UNCF, 2008; NAFEO, 2008).

One theme that emerged from the data was that of in-kind donations and services. Even the institutional officials mentioned the advantages of in –kind donations. This was also evident when the alumni mentioned mentor and tutoring programs. These programs would be advantageous to any institution. According to Independent Spector's web site (2009), the value of volunteer time is estimated at $20.25 per hour. Many grant founders are requesting such information about the number of volunteers and the dollar amount that it is equal to. This form of calculations helps with meeting financial obligations and services of proposed funding opportunities. Another aspect of fundraising is who is doing the fundraiser. It can be established from the responses that the participants in the study had a connection with a faculty member or staff member that helped them along the way while they were a student. Using the right people and voice for fundraising will benefit the fundraisers in cultivating the relationship with an alumnus.

15 IMPLICATIONS FOR POLICY AND PRACTICE

According to the literature one of the top three funding resources for institutions of higher learning is alumni giving. This general assumption is across the board for all colleges and universities. The Council for Aid to Education (2007) has reported that the top three sources for voluntary support are (1) alumni (27.8%); (2) Foundations (28.6%) and (3) Corporations (16.1%). Many HBCUs have yet to reach double digits in alumni giving (CAE, 2008; Powell, 2008; US News and World Report, 2008).

In addressing implications for policy and practice, Historically Black Colleges and Universities must be willing to re-vamp communication plans and begin to invest in other means of resource development. For instance, the research of this study revealed the often overlooked financial category of in-kind fundraising. Institutions know that they have volunteers through alumni and students but as far as accurate records of the number hours and value of donated goods and services given is often omitted (Independent Spector, 2009).

Throughout the respondents' reflections, it was surmised that HBCUs have excelled at creating the family atmosphere or the home away from home. Brown and Davis (2001) sum this up as the social capitol and contract which HBCUs were created to embellish in American society. However, this premise has not showed up in the residual effect of alumni giving back to their institution. With Tinto (1993) integration model as a guide, institutions must also ingrain as well as develop the incorporation phase of giving back financially into the students' psyche as much as the good times that they have with their colleagues. From the research data of the study it was mentioned numerous times about the pre-alumni associations as the first identified connection to alumni and also during Freshmen Orientation the purpose of alumni. It does not appear to be a concentrated effort to develop continuous, intentional delivery of information to the student body each year for students to get involve with alumni fundraising or student fundraising that is beneficial to their institution.

Fraternities and sororities and other student groups host their own fundraising programs, but the student body in general is not involved with fundraising efforts; Perhaps requiring student organizations to participate or incorporate fundraising programs that are geared to development funds for the college or university in order for them to be recognized as official organizations of the institution or to be housed on the campus. This could be in the form of student scholarships, naming rights for buildings or equipment.

A final implication for policy or practice could be the establishment of student exit plans. Students generally meet with their academic advisors to review their plans for graduation and are even required to submit electronic forms of exit from financial aid and services. These exit plans would be similar to job exit interviews when a person transitions from certain employers to new a job. Exit interviews at places of employment are created as an opportunity for the exiting employee to review what they remember about their organization or if there are any issues or problems that need to be addressed by that organization in question. This practice that is used frequently in corporate America is one that is needed in higher education settings. Students are often baffled by the graduation process or payment of services or grades to name a few, but if students were able to voice their opinions about the services they have received while a student or to submit customer survey cards about problems they may have encountered, this may be a starting point to recouping disgruntled and disconnected alumni.

Recommendations for Further Research

Historically Black Colleges and Universities have consistently championed their place in higher education. They have survived many challenges to compete in the academic arena and solidified their place as a social, political and educational icon. There are many fields yet to be conquered thus cementing a need for these institutions. This research has established a need for further research in the areas of alumni relations management that is often missing from extant literature specifically in regards to fundraising at HBCUs.

Based on some of the salient themes established in this research, further research is warranted in the areas of (1) Student perceptions of alumni at HBCUs; (2) Faculty as Fundraisers for alumni affairs and institutional advancement; (3) the effectiveness of pre-alumni clubs at HBCUs; (4) Relationship Cultivation of disgruntled and disconnected alumni.

Student perception of alumni at HBCUs

Established from the research study interviews, the perception of alumni at HBCUs was one of socialization and fellowship. Many of the alumni did not have knowledge of the duties or purpose of alumni beyond participation at events such as homecoming or football games. Some of the respondents did not have knowledge beyond ceremonial functions such as taking the oath at graduation services. Although notoriety of famous alumni may have been a factor in attending a HBCU, it was not displayed throughout the interviews the pontification of giving back that alumni are charged with doing.

Faculty as Fundraisers

Consistently mentioned in the data collection was the amalgamation of faculty being memorable as the point of contact or mentoring for many students. The purposeful and intentional utilization of faculty and staff as a bridge for cultivating relationships with former students may possibly be a missing link in fundraising that deserves further investigation. Students often remember professors and staff that assisted them in the academic choices made while attending their respective institution. The effectiveness of mentor programs or re-uniting students and faculty may also be considered an implication of policy and practice for alumni relationship building.

Effectiveness of Pre-alumni Clubs

Persistently, alumni affairs directors, development officials and alumni alike reflected on the presence of pre-alumni organizations at their institutions. Nevertheless, these organizations lack maximum exposure to the mass of students as reported by the respondents in the study. It was viewed as only a few students that participated in the activities of the club. The oxymoron of the term pre-alumni may be a deterrent for students to actively embrace the purpose of the club while a student.

Cultivating relationships with disgruntled and disconnected alumni

Although only one research participant reported discontentment upon graduating, several participants reported having knowledge of many students that left their institutions with ill feelings. This malcontent oftentimes leads to a lack of involvement post graduation. Further research into customer service and retention of alumni deserves future investigation. These untapped alumni are often not researched or contacted to try and understand what issues need to be addressed in order to avoid future failures in alumni treatment.

Conclusions

As the literature has revealed, alumni giving rates at HBCUs is relatively low as compared to predominantly white institutions. The researcher has been an active member of his alma mater's national alumni association and has been an active donor for a number of years. As an active member of an alumni association, the researcher has been engrossed in the constant challenges that face many HBCUs. Some of the assumptions that the researcher had about customer service at HBCUs were thought to become evident in the study; however, most of the respondents had positive experiences at their alma mater.

Most of the respondents in the study were believed to be loyal to their institution although this did not always result in financial donations from the alumnus. Loyalty does not always translate into dollars for HBCUs. The family atmosphere that is touted by many HBCUs would stand to reason that alumni of these institutions would give donations without any thought behind it. As altruism theory suggests, alumni should be anxious to give back and not expect anything in return. But many HBCUs lack the infra structure to compete and cultivate their alumni to become financial supporters. With a failing economy many institutions of higher learning may be faced with further financial woes as they compete with other charitable organizations to gain and retain donors. HBCUs must continue to develop their students to become active donors post graduation. The redevelopment of alumni management plans and better cultivation of alumni are imperative to the financial stability of these institutions. Nevertheless, this study adds credence to the necessary development of strong relationship building techniques that HBCUs should invest in. Further research is necessary to continued success of programs that support alumni management systems.

REFERENCES

Allen, W.R. & Jewell, J. O. (2002). A backward glance forward: past, present, and future perspectives on historically black colleges and universities. *The Review of Higher Education*, 25(3) 241 –261.

Baker, J. (2004). Impact of the student experience on alumni involvement Ed.D. Dissertation University of Central Florida United States – Florida. Retrieved May 14, 2008, from Dissertations & Theses: Full Text database. (Publication No.: AAT 3134672.)

Balderston, F. (1995). *Managing today's university: Strategies for viability, change and excellence.* San Francisco: Jossey – Bass.

Bedigian, B. (2006). Alumni Matter: Unleashing a Lifetime of Value, The Benefit of CRM Principles in the Postsecondary Environment. Hezel Associates, LLC. New York: Syracuse.

Birnbaum, R. (1988). *How colleges work. The cybernetics of academic organization and leadership.* San Francisco: Jossey – Bass. *Black Issues in Higher Education* (2004). Black college alumni gifts on the rise. 9(21).

Boulard, G. (2001). Moving toward a new era. Black issues in Higher Education, 18(9) 28, 2p.

Brown, M. (2003, January 1). Emics and Etics of Researching Black Colleges: Applying Facts And Avoiding Fallacies. *New Directions for Institutional Research,* (ERIC Document Reproduction Service No. EJ673237) Retrieved November 20, 2007, from ERIC database.

Brown, M., & Davis, J. (2001, January 1). The Historically Black College as Social Contract, Social Capital and Social Equalizer. *Peabody Journal of Education, 76*(1), 31. (ERIC Document Reproduction Service No. EJ644172) Retrieved November 20, 2007, from ERIC database.

Calvario, D. A. (1996). College Experience, satisfaction and intent to financially support one's alma mater (Doctoral dissertation, University of Northern Colorado, 1996). *Dissertation Abstracts International,* 57, 04.

Cech, S. (2008). Pressure to Lighten Tuition Burden Factors into College-Aid Equation. Education Week [serial online]. February 27, 2008; 27(25): . Available from ERIC, Ipswich, MA. Accessed May 26, 2008.

Chronicle of Higher Education (2003) Southern Association strips two black colleges of accreditation. Chronicle of Higher Education, 49(17) A34, 1/2p.

Cohen, A., (1998). The Shaping of American Higher Education: Emergence and Growth of Contemporary System. San Francisco, CA: Jossey – Bass.

Cole, D. (2008). Black Colleges Aim to Build a New History. U. S. News and World Report. http://www.usnews.com/articles/
education/best-colleges/soo8/08/21/black-colleges-aims-to-
build-a-new-history.

Council for Aid to Education (2008). www.cae.org.

Creswell, J. W., (1998). Educational Research: Planning, conducting and Evaluating Quantitative and Qualitative Research. Upper Saddle River, NJ: Prentice Hall.

Creswell, J.W. (2003). Research design: Qualitative, Quantitative, and Mixed Method approaches (2nd ed.). Thousand Oaks: Sage Publications.

Evan, A. L., Evans, V., & Evans, A. M. (2002). Historically Black Colleges and Universities (HBCUS). *Education*, 123, 3 –16.

Field, K. (2007). Philanthropist Calls on Colleges to Inspire Students to Give. Chronicle of Higher Education, 53(42). (ERIC Document Reproduction Service No EJ770985) Retrieved August 20, 2007, from ERIC database.

Fields, C. (2001). HBCUs Get Savvy about Fund Raising. *Black Issues in Higher Education,* 18(14), 38. (ERIC Document Reproduction Service No. EJ635294) Retrieved September 19, 2007, from ERIC database.

Freeman, K., & Cohen, R. (2001, January 1). Bridging the Gap between Economic Development and Cultural Empowerment: HBCUs' Challenges for the Future. *Urban Education,* 36(5ov), 585. (ERIC Document Reproduction Service No. EJ636445) Retrieved May 14, 2008, from ERIC database.

Friedmann, A. S. (2003). Building Communities of Participation through Student Advancement Programs: A First Step toward Relationship Fund raising. Ph.D dissertation, The College of William and Mary. United States – Virginia, Retrieved July, 28, 2008.

Gallo, P. J. & Hubschman, B. (2003). The Relationship between Alumni Participation and Motivation on Financial Giving. Paper presented at the Annual Meeting of the American Educational research Association (Chicago, Il, April 21-25, 2003).

Gasman, M. (2001). Racial Stereotyping in

Fundraising for Historically Black Colleges: A Historical Case Study. Paper presented at the Annual Meeting of the American Educational Research Association (Seattle, WA, April 10 – 14, 2001).

Gasman, M., Baez, B., Drezner, N., & Sedgwick, K. (2007). Historically black colleges and universities: Recent Trends. *Academe*, Jan/Feb 2007, 93(1), 69 - 77.

Grandillo, M. (1997, November). *The local College Booster Movement in Nineteenth Century Ohio.* Paper presented at the Annual meeting of the Association for the Study of Higher Education, Albuquerque, NM.

Hanson, S. K. (2000). Alumni characteristics that predict promoting and donating to alma mater: Implications for alumni relations (Doctoral dissertation, University of North Dakota, 2000). *Dissertation Abstracts International*, 61, 05A (2002): 1760.

Harris-Vasser, D., (2003) A comparative analysis of the aspects of alumni giving at public and private historically Black colleges and universities. Ed.D. dissertation, Tennessee State University, United States -- Tennessee. Retrieved May 14, 2008, from Dissertations & Theses: Full Text database. (Publication No. AAT 3116150).

Hinde, R. A. (1995). The Adaptionist approach has limits. *Psychological Inquiry: An International Journal*, 6(1), 50-51.

Holmes, G. & McElwee, G. (1995). Total Quality Management in Higher Education: How to Approach Human Resource Management. 7(6), pp. 5 – 10.

Huberman, A.M., & Miles, M.B. (2002). *The qualitative researcher's companion*. Thousand Oaks: Sage Publications.

Hunter, C. S. (1999). A study of the relationship between alumni giving and selected characteristics of alumni donors of Living Stone College, NC, *Journal of Black Issues,* 29(4) 523, 17p.

Ikenberry, J. P. (1999). Alumni institutional commitment: Connecting student involvement with alumni involvement and institutional commitment. (Doctoral Dissertation, The Pennsylvania State University, 1999) Dissertation Abstracts International, 60 07A :2042.

Independent_Sector(2009).www.independentspector. org/programs/research/ volunteer_time. html.

Journal of Blacks in Higher Education (2000). The solid alumni base of Howard University, 28, 40-41.

Journal of Blacks in Higher Education (2005). African Americans in Higher Education: Now for the Good News, http://www.jbhe.com /http://www.jbhe.com/news_views/48_blackshighe reducation.html

Journal of Blacks in Higher Education (2007). The Resuscitation of LeMoyne-Owen College, http://www.jbhe.com/latest/index082307_p.html

Johnson, J. W. & Eckel, P. D. (1998). Preparing seniors for roles as active alumni. In J. N. Gardner, G. Van der Weer, & Associates (Eds.), The Senior year experience: Facilitating integration, reflection; closure and transition (pp.227 – 241). San Francisco: Jossey – Bass Publishers.

Lackey, H.L. (2008). All Supporters Are Not members. Jackson State University National Alumni Association Weekly Presidential Newsletter Update. P10.

Marshall, C. & Rossman, G. (2006).*Designing Qualitative Research*. Thousand Oaks, CA: Sage Publications.

Mastain, L. (2007). A Phenomenological Investigation of Altruism as Experienced by Moral Exemplars. *Journal of Phenomenological Psychology*, *38*(1), 62-99. Retrieved August 29, 2008, doi:10.1163/156916207X190247.

Michael, R., Sower, V., & Motwani, J. (1997). A Comprehensive model for implementing Total Quality Management in Higher Education. *Benchmarking for Quality Management and Technology*. Bradford: 4(2) pg. 104.

Morrissey, K., & Werner-Wilson, R. (2005, Spring2005). The relationship between out-of-school activities and positive youth development: an investigation of the influences of communities and family. *Adolescence*, *40*(157), 67-85. Retrieved August 29, 2008, from Psychology and Behavioral Sciences Collection database.

Nealy, M. (2008, February 21). Alumni Giving to HBCUs Declined in 2007. *Diverse Issues in Higher Education.* 22(40), 35.

Nichols, J. (2004, March 1). Unique Characteristics, Leadership Styles, and Management of Historically Black Colleges and Universities. *Innovative Higher Education*, *28*(3), 219. (ERIC Document Reproduction Service No. EJ771435) Retrieved November 20, 2007, from ERIC database.

Palmer, T. (2002, September 1). Mending student discontent. CASE Currents, 28(7). Retrieved fromhttp://www.case.org/currents/2002/september/palmer.cfm.

Patton, M. Q. (2002). Qualitative research and evaluation methods (3rd ed.) Thousand Oaks, CA: Sage.

Powell, T. (2004, January 1). Surviving Tough Times: From Administrative Reorganizations to Finding New Streams of Revenue, Some Historically Black Colleges and Universities Are Determined to Stay Afloat. *Black Issues in Higher Education*, 20(23). (ERIC Document Reproduction Service No. Ej699890) Retrieved November 21, 2007, from Eric Database.

Ramsey, V.L. (1992). Black alum: gift of hope. Black Enterprise, 22(11) 36, 1/4p

Reaves, N. (2006). African American Alumni Perceptions regarding giving to Historically Black Colleges and Universities. Ed.D. Dissertation, North Carolina State University, United States –North Carolina. Retrieved September 19, 2007, from ProQuest Digital Dissertations database. (Publication No. AAT 3213472).

Reimer, K. (2005, July). Revisiting Moral Attachment: Comment on Identity and Motivation. *Human Development (0018716X)*, *48*(4), 262-266. Retrieved August 29, 2008, doi: 10.1159/000086861

Roach, R. (2007, February 8). The Journey for Jackson State University. *Diverse: Issues in Higher Education*, 23(26), 22. (ERIC Document Reproduction Service No. Ej764788) Retrieved November 22, 2007, from Eric Database.

Roebuck, J.B. & Murty, K.S. (1989). Historically black colleges and universities: Their Place in American Education In L.F. Goodchild & H.S. Wechsler (Eds.), *The history of higher education* (2 ed., pp. 432-458). Boston, MA: Ginn Press.

Rudolph, F. (1962). The American College and University: A History. New York: Pergamon Press.

Schervish, P. G. (1993). Taking giving seriously. In P. Dean (ed), *Taking giving seriously*. Indiana, IN

Indiana University Center on Philanthropy.

Schulze, B. S., (2005). Changing the Odds: Lessons Learned from the Kresge HBCU Initiative.

Singer, T. S. & Hughey, A. W. (2002). The role of the alumni association in student life. *New Directions for Student Services, 100*, 51 – 67.

Scott, E. (2007). Benefits of Altruism – Altruism Benefits Everyone – Here's How. www.about.com. *About.com Health's Disease and Condition content is reviewed by the Medical Review Board* updated November 24, 2007. Retrieved January 20, 2009.

Scott, L., (2001) A description of successful fund-raising units at public historically Black colleges and universities. Ph.D. dissertation, The Florida State University, United States - Florida. Retrieved May 14, 2008, from Dissertations & Theses: Full Text database. (Publica- tion No. AAT 9994577).

Smith, S. (2003). Governments and Non Profits in the Modern Age, *Society*, May / June 2003, 36 – 45.

Ramsey, V.L. (1992). Black alum: gift of hope. Black Enterprise, 22(11) 36,

Somekh, B., & Lewin, C. (2005, January 1). Research Methods in the Social Sciences. *SAGE Publications (UK)*, (ERIC Document Reproduction Service No. ED488759) Retrieved June 23, 2008, from ERIC database.

Southern Association for Colleges and Schools (2007). Southern Association for Colleges and Schools web page. Retrieved September 2007 from World Wide Web: www.sacs.org.

Southern Regional Education Board (1967). The Negro and higher education in the south. Atlanta: Commission on Higher Educational Opportunity in the South.

Strout, E. (2004). Survey notes negative Correlation between Alumni Giving and Political Commencement speeches. Chronicle of Higher Education, 51(7), p20.

Thurman, E. (2006). Performance Philanthropy: Bringing Accountability to Charitable Giving. Harvard International Review, Spring 2006, 18 – 20.

Tinto, V. (1993). Leaving college, Chicago: The University of Chicago Press.

Turner, B. (2001). Historically Black Colleges and Universities: An Educational System at the Crossroads. *Black Issues in Higher Education.* Education Resources Information Center Database, ED467333, 2001.

United Negro College Fund. (2008). www.uncf.org.

U. S. Department of Education, (2008). www.ed..gov

U.S. News and World Report (2008). Retrieved from

ww.usnews.com/sections/rankings.

Vigoda-Gadot, E. (2006, March). Compulsory Citizenship Behavior: Theorizing Some Dark Sides of the Good Soldier Syndrome in Organizations. *Journal for the Theory of Social Behaviour, 36(1), 77-93. Retrieved August 29, 2008, doi:10.1111/j.1468-5914.2006.00297.x*

Volkwein, F. J. & Parmley, K. (1999). Testing why alumni give: A model of alumni gift giving behavior. In D. Shoemaker (Ed.) Research in alumni relations.

Ward, H. (2004). The impact of collegiate involvement on African-American alumni giving. Ph.D. dissertation. Bowling Green State University United States -- Ohio: 2004. Retrieved May 14, 2008, from Dissertations & Theses: Full Text database. (Publication Number: AAT 3135447.)

Weidman, J. (1989). Undergraduate socialization: A conceptual approach. In J. Smart (Ed.), *Higher education: Handbook of theory and research* (Vol. 5). New York: Agathon.

Williams, M. & Kritsonis W. (2006). Raising More Money at the Nation's Historically Black Colleges and Universities. National Journal for Publishing and Mentoring Doctoral Student Research, 3((Capitol Campaigns. *Black Issues in Higher Education*, 18(10), 18. (ERIC Document Reproduction Service No. EJ635315) Retrieved November 21, 2007, from Eric Database.

Yates, E. L. (2001). Capital Campaigns. Black Issues in Higher Education, 18(10) 18, 8p, 7c.

ABOUT THE AUTHOR

Derek C. Henson, Ph.D. is a native of Philadelphia, MS where he was reared in a close-knit community by a socially and politically active family. Upon graduation from Philadelphia High School, Dr. Henson enrolled at Jackson State University. He was an active member of the JSU community proudly marching with the 'Sonic Boom,' enthusiastically participating in student government and excelling as a promising pre-law student. In 1991, Dr. Henson graduated from JSU with a BA in Political Science.

Soon thereafter, he began work as a teacher in Mississippi's fledgling public school system before relocating to Memphis, Tennessee where he began work with a non-profit organization. In the footsteps of his role model, Reverend Dr. Martin Luther King, Jr., Dr. Henson was determined to live a life providing social justice to the marginalized. He found both satisfaction and purpose through his work in non-profit; thus, began his Divinely Ordained vocation.

Dr. Henson, motivated by his desire to be a catalyst for positive change in the lives of those he served, graduated from the University of Memphis in 2002 with an MS in Educational Leadership and Policy Studies. The following year, he earned a certification in Urban Youth Ministries from Crichton College through the Memphis Leadership Foundation Youth Initiative. In 2009, Dr. Henson was awarded a doctorate from his alma mater Jackson State University in Urban Higher Education.

In a career spanning nearly 20 years, Dr. Henson has worked with Shelby County Head Start, Inc., Frayser Family Counseling Center and the Urban Youth Initiative. For 11 years he served as Program Director for the Metropolitan Inter-Faith Association COOL Program (College Offers Opportunities for Life). In 2014, Dr. Henson was appointed Project Director for Rescare, Inc. Workforce Services Division.

Dr. Henson has been a member of Parents for Public Schools, Arrow for Academy of Excellence, Tennessee Conference on Social Welfare (TCSW), Association for the Study of Higher Education

(ASHE) the International Review Board at the University of Memphis. He has been an vocal member of the Jackson State University Alumni Association, Inc. for nearly 30 years having served as National Second Vice President and as the current Southeast Regional Vice President. Dr. Henson is a licensed and ordained minister at New Olivet Baptist Church in Memphis, Tennessee, where he is also a member.

Dr. Henson's research, 'Institutional Relations and Their Perceived Impact on Alumni Giving at Historically Black Colleges and Universities' has been accepted for presentation by American Association of Blacks in Higher Education (AABHE) and the National Association for African American Studies (NAAAS) and Affiliates. His forthcoming project with SaFiya D. Hoskins, Ph.D., 'The Re-education of the Negro: A historical review of Carter G. Woodson's epic work' will be published spring 2015.

www.DrDerekHenson.com

DEREK C. HENSON, PH.D.

www.ubiquitouspress.com

Made in the USA
Columbia, SC
21 November 2024

47158004R00087